Peking Cooking

PEKING COOKING

by
Kenneth H. C. Lo

WITH A FOREWORD BY
WILLIAM EMPSON

PANTHEON BOOKS
A Division of Random House, New York

Library of Congress Cataloging in Publication Data

Lo, Kenneth H. C.
Peking Cooking.

   1. Cookery, Chinese. 2. Peking — Restaurants,
lunch rooms, etc. I. Title.
TX724.5.C5L6   1973   641.5'951   72-11556
ISBN 0-394-48502-5

Manufactured in the United States of America
FIRST AMERICAN EDITION

To Number One Brother, Charles Hsiao Chao Lo,
with whom I shared so much during my
five sunlit years in Peking.

Contents

Contents

PART THREE
HOME-COOKED AND OTHER DISHES

Foreword

BY WILLIAM EMPSON

I did not realise the eminence of Chinese food in the eyes of the world till I went to a teaching job in Tokyo, in 1931. I had much enjoyed the Chinese food in Soho, but in those days Soho just went in for providing the foods of all nations, and there was nothing to make you consider what they thought of one another's cuisines. Whereas, in Tokyo, one of the things a prominent Japanese would think it standard to tell the press, on his return from some bout of foreign travel, was that Chinese food was of course the best in the world. The Japanese would not have said this unless they considered it too obvious to be hidden, though no doubt they felt that their generosity here excused their slanging the Chinese in every other department, and gave a pleasant snub to the Europeans. The English colony in Tokyo was inclined to say that the Japanese only kept alive by eating Chinese food secretly in their kitchens; but after I had been introduced to the skiing hotels, which were largely patronised by very poor students, I realised that they too could produce comforting restorative food. In both countries the soya bean, not any animal, was the main source of oil; but in Japan the ascetic military tradition made it good-class to serve meals with none. The Ginza, the main street of Tokyo, was like Soho in offering the cuisines of all nations, and I was pleased to find that the largest and most popular eating-house, the one that provided American food, was the only one to offer Chop Suey. I was reminded of this long after when I had to stay a night or two in Shanghai at one of the grim international hotels which then (perhaps 1948) catered for Europeans, and got talking at the bar to a rather gloomy American tycoon; I said something about the marvellous range of the restaurants of the city – you understand, it was enough for them to offer the cuisines of all the provinces of China. 'Yeah', he said. 'Y'know, what makes me feel bad is that I actually like Chinese chow'. I fell silent, out of reverence for his loyalty; clearly, he meant the food of China-town in San Francisco. A very nice place too, but it did seem a long way from Shanghai.

In America, you understand, the Chinese themselves had devel-oped a special cuisine to suit the taste of the natives, just as eighteenth-century Canton developed a sheer school of bogus chinoiseries which could only be sold to Europeans. With the same energetic ingenuity, but the other way round, Peking had two restaurants supplying two different kinds of Mongol food, cooked by the customer over a naked fire in each case, but one dry and the other wet; unknown in Mongolia, I was told, but a kind of poetical idealisation of what nomads might do after a hard day keeping the animals on the move. The dry one needed chop-sticks four feet long and special wood to burn under a grill; it would be much admired in London, but the fire laws prevent it. . . . I should add, come to think of it, that I haven't been to San Francisco since 1950, and very likely it has genuine Chinese cooking by now. Certainly London's new Chinatown in Gerrard Street near Piccadilly is fiercely genuine, a most fortunate acci-dental result of our sad muddle about London; and this is not sur-prising, as most of the clients are themselves Chinese. The most difficult thing about running a good restaurant, one is always told, is to keep the cooks from losing heart; a new place, you will find, is nearly always serving better food than it will later on. But in Gerrard Street the cooks are cheek by jowl, and liable to taste one another secretly; and the food strikes me as wonderfully genuine and various, though of course it does not set out to repre-sent all provinces.

An important fact about Chinese food was thrust into my mind in 1937, when I was part of the grand motorcade of a Minister of Chiang-Kai-Shek's Government who was escaping from the Japanese by a retreat through Changsha, Nanning etc. into French Indochina. (The night before reaching the frontier, we were all issued with bogus certificates for the injections demanded by the French, so it really did feel grand.) They have a delicious citron fruit there called pumelo, a parent of the grape-fruit I was told, like an orange but large and with a very thick pulpy white rind just under the skin. We were enjoying these in the heat and throwing the skin onto the road from the motor-cars, and I noticed a wrinkled old hag who was picking it all up. What a horrible thing it is, I felt for a moment, to close one's eyes to such desperate misery as must be going on all around us. But that same evening, when we were feasted as usual at a sprawling ramshackle hotel, the rind of the pumelo was served, reduced to human food in some magical way with a thick encouraging sauce, and it was agreed to be one of the best things we were given. The old woman did not collect this stuff because she was starving, but because it was a delicacy which somebody in her house knew how to cook. The peasantry in China expect to eat well, when things are normal, and hold varying opinions about how to do it. I must not be ignorantly cheerful; someone wrote that there has been a famine in one province or another of China every ten years since the time of Confucius; but in your own province this would only work out as once in every two or three generations. In between whiles there has long been a broad-based satisfaction about food, not easy to match elsewhere in Asia, or indeed in the whole human story.

I realised this more confidently in 1950, on my return from an American Summer School to a now Communist China; it turned out that the railway was being improved, so that, after exhausting examination and query, the visitors were carried right through Tientsin and dumped at a wayside station for further indefinite delay. My wife had cleverly succeeded in meeting the boat, and soon found that, where the road branched off to join the station, we had a tiny local restaurant. It did not have the shop-finish that we are accustomed to think hygienic; the floor was earth, the benches bare wood, the ceiling darkened by smoke. But the food made me feel at once that it was wonderful to be back again, and so did the Erh Kwo Toe, the local raw spirit twice distilled; though I had been living very comfortably on my Norwegian tramp steamer. Most of the passengers, as I remember, were Scandinavian diplomats, and it took a lot of coaxing before they would regard this stuff as even possible food, though they were

Notes on the Recipes

The recipes, unless otherwise specified, are sufficient for 4-6 persons when served in conjunction with three or four other dishes.

Gourmet powder is monosodium glutamate. Although several countries continue to use this additive quite regularly and without worry, it has been the subject of much controversy in the United States. Scientists and consumer groups warn of possibly serious physiological effects, plus the transitory symptoms of Chinese Restaurant Syndrome and mild allergies; manufacturers of baby foods have discontinued its use; yet the Food and Drug Administration asserts that there is no scientific proof of deleterious effects and maintains MSG's classification as a permissible food additive. No taste-enhancer should be necessary, however, if you are cooking with good, fresh ingredients and serving them right away.

Caster sugar is superfine granulated sugar.

Introduction

To write about Peking's food and cooking one has to write about Peking itself, for they are such an integral part of the city's life. Few places in the world have generated as many memories or as must nostalgia as the 'Old Capital' of China (an expression of endearment, since Peking is now so new); and a good percentage of all the reminiscences is no doubt occasioned by its food, since it has undeniably added much to the colour and character of Peking's lively, unique scene.

What is it, then, that is so remarkable about Peking? What has captured and charmed the imagination of countless generations—from Chinese poets and writers of old, to Marco Polo in the fourteenth century, down to more recent travellers to the Capital of the People's Republic of China?

Part of the attraction could be Peking's climate, though certainly not its geographical situation—except that being just south of arid Inner Mongolia, it does appear, if approached from the north, to have the lushness of an oasis. Otherwise, as a city, it is not built on picturesque hills like Athens or Edinburgh, nor around bustling busy rivers like London, Paris or Vienna, nor is it situated at the gateways of great oceans like New York, or San Francisco. For Peking is built simply on a flat plain (the blue Western Hills being some twelve to fifteen miles to the west). Perhaps it is this very lack of topographical distraction together with the remarkable dryness and clarity of the air, which accounts for its extraordinarily bright sunshine during the day and brilliant moonlight at night. These have left an indelible imprint on the minds of all who have lived and immersed themselves in the life of Peking.

Maybe, too, it is the flatness of the land which induces a feeling of grandeur and dimension – the mariners' awareness of the vast-ness of the ocean all around –, which somehow brings the indivi-dual closer to the elements, in this case to the vastness of the sky and land. In Peking one is aware that from here where one stands, the land rolls westwards unceasingly across the great expanse of the Chinese interior, over the highlands and mountains of Singkiang, along the plateau of Central Asia, across the Caspians, the Russian Steppes, and the countries and lands of Eastern Europe, all the way, non-stop, to the Atlantic seaboard. As one scans the horizon, one cannot but sense a feeling of 'from here to Eternity'. This is enhanced by the fact that in Peking one continually lives in proximity with a crumbling decaying history which goes back to the very birth of man: one is conscious that the sun is shining down from an ancient sky, and that the moon-light which shines down at night has thrown similar shadows in similar courtyards for tens of centuries. All this causes one to be very aware of the grandeur of both time and space in which one is existing. They are some of the ingredients which add up to the essence of Peking.

Of Peking's many magnificences, a notable one is its food. Once, three years ago, I defined it as, 'The crystallisation of the many inventions and performances of the generations of Imperial chefs of the different dynasties which have ruled in Peking for nearly a millennium, and the grass-root dishes of the locality which the people of Shangtung and Hopei have been in the habit of preparing, together with all the culinary contributions which have flowed in from the far-flung regions and provinces of China, and which over the years have established their reputation in the Old Capital. Peking cooking is, in short, the top table of Chinese culinary art.' Looking at the definition again today I find no reason to alter it.

THE CHARACTER AND ENVIRONMENTS OF PEKING COOKING

As intimated in the 'definition', Peking cooking derives from four distinct backgrounds: firstly there is the local cooking of Shangtung and Hopei (in which province Peking is situated), which makes extensive use of local products such as the 'Great White Cabbage' (Chinese celery cabbage), leeks, tomatoes, onions, garlic, ginger, and scallion (spring onion), cucumber, bean paste and bean sauce, together with plenty of pork, chicken, giant prawns (a product of the Gulf of Chili); then there is the Chinese Moslem cooking of Inner Mongolia and Singkiang, which specialises in roasting, barbecuing and deep-boiling lamb, beef and duck, all eaten with piquant 'dips' and 'mixes' of seasonings and sauces; then there are the more refined and elaborate dishes which come from the Imperial Palace kitchens, many of which employ a good dosage of sugar, as the last powerful Empress of China, the Empress Dowager, was a sweet-toothed old woman. (If Peking cooking has been influenced at all by Manchuria, whose cooking has few distinctive features, it was through the Palace, for the last dynasty was Manchurian.) And finally, there is the cooking of the Lower Yangtze (Yangchow, Nanking, Soochow, Shanghai, Hangchow); of the south, which comprises Fukien and Kwang-tung (Canton); and from the one province in the west, Szechuan.

Although these styles of cooking are all represented in Peking, it is the local cooking of Hopei and Shangtung and the Moslem cooking which dominate. The cuisines of the Yangtze, the south and the west may appeal to connoisseurs and cosmopolitans, but they made little impression on local taste. These styles are support-ed and patronised by mainly the 'expatriates' of the 'Outer Provinces'. The Pekingese themselves would sample them only for a change or out of curiosity. Because of their self-absorption and their disinclination to lift their gaze, they have developed a 'provincialism' in their taste which is not unlike the provincialism of which Londoners are often accused.

But the food situation in Peking is very unlike that of London, where the catering scene is flooded with foreign fare, such as French, Italian, Chinese and Indian food, and where genuine English cooking is hard to come by; in Peking the eating scene is dominated almost entirely by local fare: by the indigenous Hopei, Shangtung, Moslem and Palace styles of cooking. One might have to look hard for the fourth style before locating it. But if one were to search hard enough one could find not only food from the 'Outer Provinces', but French, Russian, English or even German cooking of a reasonable standard. This variety is what makes the Peking eating scene so intriguing. And with everything hidden away in the narrow 'hutungs', the search itself becomes part of the excitement. On the whole, however, one is naturally surrounded by what are indigenous Peking dishes. Ranging from 'small eats' to major banquet dishes, they form a characteristic world of their own, a world which reflects all the varied aspects of life and seasons in Peking with all the characteristic flavours that linger so long after savouring them.

When thinking of Peking cooking, one often envisages the typical surroundings in which it is served and eaten. In Peking there are no tall private buildings; none was allowed to rival even remotely the height of the Imperial roofs. Most of the more opulent residences are single-storey structures built behind high walls, around a series of rectangular courtyards. The entrances and structures of the larger *first-class* Peking restaurants are no different from the residences. They too are built on one storey, behind high walls with lacquered gates, and contain a number of interconnecting courtyards. The name of the patron entering the restaurant is announced at the front gate, and shouted from one courtyard to another until he and his party are found a private room or a partitioned-off area for their feasting. Unlike Western restaurants, where everybody eats within sight of one another, in Peking restaurants each group dines in privacy, although people are fully aware of all the other parties which are going on in either the same courtyard, or the next room or just behind the partition. There is visual seclusion but no aural seclusion at all. Indeed, all the instructions for the meal seem to be said extra loud in traditional Chinese restaurants. The orders given by the patrons are sometimes shouted right across several courtyards to the kitchen, which may be fifty yards away; this seems to be done when the dishes ordered are particularly noble and expensive dishes: the names of the dishes are then made particularly distinct and impressive for everybody within earshot. Occasionally this is also done when dishes ordered are notably undistinguished–to the consternation of the customer concerned – such as 'Two Fried Eggs'. The Pekingese word for eggs is 'Dan'. When that dish is shouted across courtyards it seems to ring a long time in the air, which makes it particularly disconcerting to the customer!

All this shouting, intermixed with laughter and conversation, and all the sizzling of the stir-frying, and the dull thud of the explosive-frying ('Po'), together with the banging and scraping which goes on in the kitchen, whose windows, belching with steam and smoke, face the courtyard, make the Peking restaurant a very lively place indeed. Some of the courtyards are equipped with stages or platforms suitable for operatic or theatrical entertainments. These are put on for special occasions, such as weddings, birthdays, anniversaries and other celebrations, when a specially large party would occupy a whole courtyard. What with music being played, and actors impersonating women screeching at the tops of their voices, it all adds to the general din and mêlée, which gives an impression of an oriental pop session getting 'high', drunk on its own food, drink and noise. Yet beneath the surface, everything is conducted with the order, politeness and dignity that distinguishes life in Peking.

According to a well-known authority on Peking food, Wu Shih Fu, who writes a regular column on Peking cooking in the *Hong Kong News*, some of the largest Peking restaurants, in which he and his relatives had worked for several generations, consisted of over ten courtyards or well over 100,000 square feet. These are known as 'Fang Tsung', or 'Food Establishments'. The smaller ones are called 'Fang Diàn', ('Food Shops'), or 'Chiu Ch'a' ('Wine Houses'). The latter are perhaps one category higher than 'T'sa Guan' ('Tea Houses') where no large major courses are served, but only snacks. Because of the lack of pubs, bars and coffee houses, the 'Wine Houses', and 'Tea Houses' play an important part in the life of the Chinese people.

A unique place in Peking is the East Market. The only way to describe it is to say that it combines something of Soho, Covent Garden and the Portobello Road, for you can purchase live pets, old prints and books, cabbages, sweets and fruits, as well as attend theatres or operas there. Note that theatres and operas are in the plural, as several of these activities go on at the same time. The market also, of course, is thronged with small eating-places, as well as boasting several famous restaurants (we shall come to them and savour their dishes later in the book).

Many of the walls in this shopping and entertainment concourse are packed with Chinese confectioneries, especially with a great range of fruit glacés and crystallised fruits, which can rival the best offered in the West. In the preparation of Chinese food, many of these preserved fruits go into the making of various sweet soups, sweet congees (soft rice), and such puddings as the 'Eight Precious Rice'.

The numerous small eating-places in the Market make it so convenient for people to rest their feet and have a light meal in between bouts of shopping or entertainment, or in between simply browsing in bookstalls or antique shops hoping to dig up some treasure. Here in the Market there are also, apart from operas and theatres, cinemas and amusement halls. One can indulge one's sensual inclinations to the full without ever leaving this one covered area. It is one of our Chinese habits of having all our fun and games in one grand conglomeration. The only thing which is not now available are the brothels, which used to be situated not too far away in an area called the 'Pa Ta Hutungs'. The 'hutungs' are the city lanes, and the 'Pa Ta Hutungs' are the 'Eight Big Famous City Lanes' (or infamous!), where food was provided or could be sent for from nearby restaurants. These 'hutungs' were in the main very respectable residential lanes (corresponding to London's Georgian terraces). The unpaved streets were banked in by high walls. But behind them all the goings-on in Peking were taking place. In the days when I was a student there, in between the demos. and clashes with the gendarmes (for we were the original and earliest 'student rebels'!), we used to cycle or ride in rickshaws between the 'hutungs'. As Peking is very dry for most of the year, the surface of the streets in the 'hutungs' appeared to consist of powdered dust, and the rickshaws moved through them quite noiselessly. The pullers wore soft cloth-soled shoes, and as they strode or trotted along, there seemed to be no sound except for the barely audible steady thump of their cloth-soles on the powdered dust as we proceeded along the lanes in the day or at night. Whatever may have been the occurrences of the day, which were occasionally rough, we would usually end up consuming a hearty meal in one of the 'hutungs', behind the high walls, whether it were in a restaurant or a residence. To ride back again in the middle of the night, through the crisp air, and again noiselessly through the 'hutungs', often with moonlight shining down with marvellous brilliance from above, throwing shadows of the walls and barren winter leaves into deep relief, left sensations which are never to be forgotten. Occasionally at corners of these 'hutungs' one met food-vendors, still plying their wares in the middle of the night, their mobile stalls (carried on their shoulders when moving) lit by a couple of oil-lamps. We sometimes stopped and had a hot soup. which was always welcomed as a night-cap in the sub-zero winter. There are a few recipes in this book, which are derived from these food-vendors, some of whom over the years have become landmarks of the 'Old Capital'.

What was surprising about Peking was that often behind those ancient façades, dust-paved streets, half-decayed walls and faded lacquered gates, the rooms and residence were surprisingly modern. Besides the rockeries and lily ponds in the courtyards, the rooms were often centrally heated; there were sunken baths with showers in tiled bathrooms, and I have even known sprung dance-floors which could hold a hundred in private houses. Of course, these were the exceptions. In a majority of cases, the courtyards, rooms, furniture behind the walls were as dilapidated as the walls themselves. But in this general decay there was often a lingering spirit of indulgence and largesse, and in this spirit the food was often very good. I have had some excellent food in Peking in some of the most decayed buildings!

Perhaps this spirit of munificence derived from the tradition of Imperial days, which were after all not so distant when counted in the life-span of Peking. The Republic was installed in 1912 and the People's Republic only came into being in 1949. After the Liberation many of the well-known chefs from the Imperial Palace kitchens were brought or invited back into service from retirement (the majority were in their seventies and eighties) in order that their skill and methods could be noted, so that this aspect of our 'national heritage' would not be lost.

It is well known that many Chinese maestros tended to keep something of their own art to themselves, and they were even careful or reluctant in imparting some of their innermost secrets to their heir or pupils. During the first half of the 1950s, time was almost running out for some culinary records to be made. It was the establishment of a number of eating establishments in Pai Hai ('North Sea') Park, which specialised in dishes which were 'after the Style of the Imperial Kitchen', which has enabled us today to have more to go on than just word of mouth. Many of the ex-Imperial chefs were 'brought to life' again at a very advanced age. It is due to them that we now have a fairly precise idea of what the 'Court Dishes' were.

From what we can now glean, it would appear that the catering in the Imperial Palaces during the last dynasty was more impressive for its scale than for its inventiveness or refinement. This becomes more apparent when one reads the memoirs of the last Emperor of China, Pu-Yi, who died only a few years ago in Peking, when he was serving as a gardener in the Botanical Gardens under the People's Republic, and was quite proud of his green fingers. In reading his memoirs, I was fascinated by his account of the meals he used to have. 'Of all the "shows" which went on in the Forbidden City one of the most wasteful of material and labour was food,' he wrote. 'There was no particular time at which the Emperor's meals were served. It was all up to the Emperor to indicate his wishes and give the order. As soon as I gave the order "serve the meal" the order was relayed by a chain of court officials and attendants, which echoed through the halls of the palace until it reached the appropriate kitchen. Then before the echo had died away, a troop of several scores of attendants would start to move out of the kitchen in a crocodile file each bearing a dish. At the same time another group of attendants would bring in seven tables, together with various red-lacquered boxes and gold-decorated food containers. In the spring and autumn all the foods would be contained in china dishes of "Imperial Yellow", bearing the sign "Ten Thousand Longevity of

Limitless Frontier". In the winter the food would be contained in silver dishes and bowls, superimposed on china or porcelain hot-water containers. A silver disc is placed in the food in every dish to indicate that it is unadulterated and unpoisoned. At the same time for the same reason each of the dishes would be tried and tasted first of all by a court official. Thereupon an announcement would be made "remove the 'lids' (discs)" when 4–5 of the attendants would pick up the discs from all the dishes, and place them on a large plate to be taken away. Whereupon I would commence my meal.'

For a normal meal, the Empress Dowager would have one hundred main dishes placed on six tables. 'When it came to my time I had only some thirty odd dishes. An account sheet (menu) which I found, dated during the second month of the fourth year of my reign (or the Third Month of the Third Year of the Republic) stated that I had the following for breakfast:

"Chicken with Mushrooms, Duck with 'Triple Fish', Stewed Liver & Lung, Shredded Chicken with Five Ingredients, Stewed Tender Pork, Sliced Pork with Celery Cabbage, Red Cooked Lamb, Lamb Cooked with Spinach and Bean Curd, Walnut & Taro, Barbecued Meat with White Cabbage, Mutton simmered with Carrot, Slivers of Duck Cooked with Bêche de mer, Quick-Fried Diced Duck Cubelets, Fairy Rice, Red Cooked Mushrooms, Sliced Pork Cooked with Sliced Bamboo-shoots, Shredded Lamb stewed with Shredded Cow-heel, Deep-Fried Spring Rolls, Sliced Pork Quick Fried with Yellow flower Greens, Smoked Pork Knuckles, Cooked Egg Plant, Shredded Cabbage Stir-Fried with Chili Oil, Five Flavoured Meat, Sacrificial Sliced Pork Soup, White-Cooked Long-Simmered Beef, White Cooked Pork." They seemed to have made no distinction between breakfast food and any other meal.'

'All these foods were, in fact, all ready-cooked and kept on the stove, otherwise they could not possibly have been made ready at a moment's command. The court officials knew that since the days of Emperor Kwang Hsu, the Emperor had never relied on these vast spreads for his daily succor.'

The Emperor Pu-Yi's own comment on the official food that

he was receiving was, 'One big tasteless spread. All show and no flavour! All elaboration and no substance! All expense and no result!'

The food which he actually ate came either from the kitchen of the Empress or from those of his Royal Concubines, each one of whom had one or more excellent chefs, who would prepare at each mealtime some twenty first-class succulent dishes for the Emperor.

According to a household account sheet, dated the Third Year of His Reign, the total amount of meat and poultry consumed by his royal family of six for that year was: 3,960 pounds of meat (one Chinese 1lb then would be about $1\frac{1}{4}$–$1\frac{1}{2}$lb nowadays) and 388 ducks and chickens!

The surprising thing was that in spite of all this unparalleled extravagance, the contribution of the Palace to Peking cooking as a whole is not nearly as great as the contribution made by Chinese Moslem cooking, which is basically much more rough and ready (after all it was derived from the nomadic life of the grasslands and deserts). For nearly a third of all the better-known restaurants in Peking seemed to have been Chinese Moslem restaurants.

The Chinese Moslem population resides in a belt of land stretching westwards from Peking through Inner Mongolia towards Central Asia. Their food has the distinct flavour of these vast open spaces, of the steppes and highlands, where cattle and cattle-meats form the main bulk of their diet. The meat is often cooked lengthily in big chunks, or alternatively it is sliced paper-thin and cooked almost instantaneously by a quick dip in boiling broth or given a few turns over a blazing barbecue. Both types of meats being simply cooked, are doused before eating, in 'dips' and 'mixes' of sauces and seasonings which are placed in small dishes on the table. This type of simply-cooked meat (like the roast beef of Britain) appears to have the most lasting appeal not only for the Moslems but to all who have savoured it. The dishes have now become accepted features of Peking. The famous 'Peking Duck', the 'Peking Hot Pot', the various table-barbecues, where sliced lamb and beef are cooked over a blazing brazier placed on a rough-topped table, all have a common Moslem background.

The apparent strong Moslem-Mongolian influence is easily understood. For the Mongols were once–in the time of Marco Polo, during the Great Yuan Dynasty–rulers in Peking. It was they who laid out the plan of the city. Besides, when living in Peking, you feel that Mongolia is just behind in the 'backyard'. When the seasonal winds blow with the change of seasons, the sandstorms, from Inner Mongolia cover Peking as thickly as fog used to cover London. For you need only travel north-eastwards for a mere forty miles before you get to the Great Wall, which appears to have been an emotional dividing line between China and Mongolia. It was originally built two centuries before Christ to keep out the Tartar hordes from the North (Mongolia-Siberia), and it has since been serving the same purpose intermittently through the dynasties and centuries. When we stood on top of the Great Wall, which we used to visit on picnics, all the areas to the north appeared barren and arid, and already the land seemed to be rising to the uplands of Mongolia. South of the Wall, the land appeared much more lush and habitable. In point of fact, from where we were it was still a good distance to Inner Mongolia. You would have to get as far as Kalgan, which is at least another 120 miles to the north-west. It used to require two locomotives, or an extra large and powerful one, to haul the train up to the plateau, where at different points in history the rough-riding hordes from the north used to pour in on Peking. And with them they brought in their course, unrefined, unsophisticated style of cooking, which Peking has now adopted as one of its own most refined, distinctive and sophisticated styles of food.

For vegetarian cooking in Peking we used to have to go to the temples and monasteries, for vegetarian foods are the speciality of the Buddhists. In the blue line of Western Hills, which are about twelve to fifteen miles west of Peking, nestled numerous small and medium-sized temples and monasteries; there was the Jade Fountain Temple, the Reclining Buddha Temple, the Chieh Tai Monastery, Tang Chieh Monastery, and many others. Some of these places even served European food (at 80 cents, or about 43p for three courses)! But, of course, they were best for their own vegetarian cuisine, although this was seldom of the most elaborate kind. But vegetarian food could also be had in most restaurants, if requested; the principles of cooking being much the same as any other type of Chinese food. The total weight of its influence on Peking food and cooking is, however, much less than, say, Moslem cooking. It could be that in the cold climate of the north there is a natural propensity to richer and more meaty foods.

The presence of all the various styles of southern foods, which in their own domains have enormous repertoires, is felt in Peking, but not very markedly. There were a score or so of restaurants which purveyed them. One would talk of visiting a Cantonese restaurant, or eating some Szechuanese food for a change, or having some Yangtse food (what we called Huai-Yang cuisine); of trying the dishes of Huai River and City of Yangchow, or Su-Chieh cuisine, or the food of Kiangsu and Chekiang (in which Soochow, Hangshow, Nanking and Shanghai were situated) just as one would talk these days of having Greek food, Japanese food or Scandinavian food in London. However, they were features of Peking which added spice to the gastronomic scenery. Over the decades some of the restaurants did become very well known, and their styles of cooking did have at least a creeping influence on the local culinary attitudes (which the southerners considered as narrow and slightly bigoted). At least the locals became aware that there were other styles of cooking in China, as refined and per-haps with even more impressive repertoires, since the range of seafoods and vegetables available in the south was much greater. Many southern gourmets I know regard Peking cooking as next to that of the Siberian Tartars!

The main bulk of foods consumed in Peking are, naturally, items of local produce, prepared in a style which can only be styled as North China, the chief centres of which are the provinces of Hopei and Shangtung, with Shensi and Manchuria making but small contributions. Historically speaking, what is surprising is that in spite of Manchuria's size (half of the whole of Europe) and three centuries of Manchurian rule, which immediately preceded the Republic, Manchu cooking has on its own contri-buted so little to Peking cooking. One can only presume that there was no clearly defined style of cooking in Manchuria except for what has been brought there by the immigrants from North China.

Being based mainly on local produce, Peking food is naturally very reflective of the seasons. As soon as the autumn was upon us the giant pears were on the stalls in the market, followed by the orange-red persimmons. The winter scene is dominated by the 'Great White Cabbage', a vegetable of such distinctive appeal and flavour that a mere suggestion of it sends one immediately back in mind to North China. It is also a most versatile vegetable, capable of the most delicate as well as the simplest and roughest of treatments. In the winter they are often seen laid out or piled up in the courtyard or open passageways, where they are half covered by drifting dirt and dust. But the latter washes off as easily as soil and dirt fall from celery when put under running water. Once washed they are gleaming white, with a suggestion of ivory and green to denote their bud-like vegetable freshness. The number of ways in which this 'cabbage' can be appealingly cooked are innumerable. Another typical item of the season are the giant prawns which appeared to be fattest and most plentiful in the winter. They are almost the size of small lobsters – between three and six inches or so in length. When cooked they curl up and turn bright red. One of the favourite ways of preparing them is to fry them almost dry, with a small amount of chopped onion, ginger and garlic and dry salted beans in a little oil. The use of these strong-tasting vegetables is very widespread in North China. Unlike many other countries where prawns and lobster are regarded as high-class delicacies available only in establishments of fashion or pretension, in Peking giant prawns were available in road-side cafés and village restaurants – they could, in fact, be had almost anywhere.

The charcoal-burning hot-pot, another characteristic sight of Peking, appeared on the dinner table with the arrival of winter. As the charcoal blazed in the fat central funnel of the hot-pot, the soup and food in the encircling 'moat' bubbled and boiled. When the lid was lifted off such a pot as it was brought in from the kitchen, the steam and delectable smell rose to the ceiling with all the drama of the dreaded mushroom cloud. But in this case the fall-out was mouthwatering. The presence of this hot-pot–a kind of culinary nuclear oven–added to the warmth and liveliness of any family gathering.

Winter is, of course, the greatest eating season. When winter started to slip away and there was a feeling that spring was just around the corner, it was time for 'spring rolls'. These are pancake rolls, which the diners themselves roll at the table. Into them are added a wide variety of stuffings, mainly vegetables and shredded meats: either savoury and hot fillings which have just come out of the pan, or raw or lightly-cooked vegetables which are crunchy and thus add a new dimension to the general texture. The meat most often used is lamb (shredded), and the vegetable, 'Chiu T'sai', which has a taste somewhere between bean sprouts and chives. These were often joined by shredded cucumber, radishes and spring onion, all heavily brushed with plum sauce and various types of sweetened bean pastes to give that added piquancy.

When summer was with us there was a great harvest of fruits and vegetables. There were plentiful peaches, apples and grapes in North China. Peking even had strawberries. The dominating vegetable in the summer seemed to be tomatoes, which in season crept into many dishes. They were sometimes served stuffed in a variety of ways.

In the summer fresh-water crabs became nearly as plentiful as prawns in winter. There were restaurants which specialised in crabs, where they were simply steamed; their meat was dipped before eating in a mixture of vinegar and ginger, and the feet and claws were chewed and sucked–these were hammered last, and their meat extracted. You ate until you had built up a mountain of shells on the table.

Throughout the year, of course, you could have all the pork, lamb, beef, duck and chicken dishes. Often in some areas of the city, or immediately outside, the ponds or artificial lakes were drained, and then you suddenly had an over-supply of fresh fish in the vicinity; otherwise the Yellow River Carp which had always been so much extolled, was in the opinion of all the southerners I knew, very much over-rated. The fascination of Peking has many aspects. I hope in this book to be able to present something of its culinary charm.

Kenneth Hsiao Chien Lo
February 1970

PART ONE

Methods and Ingredients Peculiar to Peking Cooking

The ingredients and methods used in Chinese cooking are as a rule employed fairly generally throughout China. There are a number, however, which are more characteristic of one locality than another. The following are definitely more characteristic of Peking than of anywhere else. They are no doubt traceable to the conjunction of geography and history as well as to accidents, which seem always to feature quite largely in human evolution. But when one examines the ingredients and the methods of heating, one finds that only in some cases can the two be considered separately; in the majority they are so inextricably connected that they must be considered merely as different aspects of the same thing. Hence when one considers certain heating methods one would invariably accept that certain ingredients must go with them. As far as ingredients are concerned, when a Chinese considers Peking cooking he will invariably think of the three strong-flavoured vegetables – onion, garlic and ginger – which are so universal in North China cooking (which also makes the northerner seem somewhat smelly to the southerner!); he will also think of the Great White Cabbage, which can be produced in the form of so many palatable dishes, both homely and banquet-worthy; he will think too of roasting by hanging in a kiln-like brick oven – as in the roasting of Peking Duck. The latter method, like deep-boiling, is what Peking has inherited from the Chinese Moslem and Mongolian cooking. What are the other methods and ingredients which Peking has inherited from its historical and geographical past? In the average Chinese mind this question is bound to produce a confusion of images. The following enumeration of methods of preparation

33

and heating, as well as of the ingredients which go with them, is an attempt to tabulate them so that they will not be continually confused with other perhaps very similar methods employed in North China and elsewhere.

In the West, Chinese cooking seems to be solely identified with the practice of 'Stir-Frying', which is undoubtedly peculiarly Chinese. In point of fact, however, almost all methods of heating popularly used in the West are also used extensively in China: such as casserole-cooking, stewing, barbecuing, grilling, griddle-cooking, poaching, boiling, deep-boiling, deep-frying, shallow-frying, steaming, double-boiling. And because of the Chinese practice of multi-phase cooking in which several methods of heating are successively employed the variations in overall heating methods are much greater than is usual in the West. It is when multi-phase heating is married to multi-phase flavouring that the permutations border on the magical and mysterious. The following identification parade of some of the familiar terms used in Peking cooking is an attempt to unravel some of the magic and mystery and to show that the methods employed are much less complicated than they are thought to be.

1. *Bāo* is one of the most dominant characteristics of Peking cooking. In the mind of the average Chinese, 'Bāo' is a form of stir-frying. In point of fact it embraces more than cooking in oil, as shown by the following main varieties of 'Bāo'. The term can perhaps be best rendered as 'Sizzling', but it can also embrace rapid cooking in water or broth.

(a) *Chiang Bāo* means to sizzle in bean paste. Here the cooking is in a form of two-phase heating: first of all the principal material–meat or poultry–is diced into approximately $\frac{1}{2}''$ cubelets and lightly battered (with egg and cornflour). They are then deep-fried or fried in ample oil for 1–4 minutes and drained.

The bean paste is then fried and stirred with a small amount of oil in another pan with a small amount of supporting flavours such as a few teaspoons of sugar, sherry, chopped onion, garlic and onion. The mixture is slowly mixed and stir-fried until most of the moisture has evaporated. It is

34

then that the principal material (diced meat) is re-introduced into the dish to take on the layer of thick bean paste sauce which gives the dish its character. This last phase is a proper 'stir-fry', where the diced meat is turned and stirred vigorously in the bean paste sauce over high heat, usually for under 1 minute.

(b) *Yien Bāo* or 'Salt Sizzling' is a triple-heating process for diced meat and poultry. It consists of first of all immersing the meat cubelets in boiling water for a minute or two and then, after draining, deep-frying (or semi-deep-frying) them for another minute or two. Then they are put aside and kept warm for the final process.

This consists of frying chopped onion and garlic in a small amount of oil, with the addition of a tablespoonful or two of chicken broth, sherry, coriander and finally salt. The diced meat which has been deep-fried and drained is added into the pan and stir-fried vigorously over high heat for a matter of $\frac{1}{2}$–1 minute before serving.

(c) *Chung Bāo* or 'Onion Sizzling' is a straightforward single-heating stir-fry. It consists usually of using approximately equal amounts of onion and meat. The latter is generally cut into strips or slices and marinated in soya sauce, sherry and gourmet powder. The oil used in frying is usually lard with a little sesame oil added in the end. The onion is sliced thin and stir-fried for a couple of minutes in a few tablespoons of lard. The meat is then added and the stir-frying continued for a further 2–3 minutes over high heat when a small amount of vinegar and sesame oil is added. After a final stir-up with these two final ingredients, the dish is served.

(d) *Tang Bāo* or 'Broth Sizzling' is a double-heating process of cooking; the ingredients are cut up very fine, dipped in boiling water for a couple of minutes and then thoroughly drained. They are then marinated in a mixture of salt, soya sauce, sherry, gourmet powder, sesame oil, shrimp oil and chilli oil, including some chopped coriander, chilli pepper and spring onion. When the food is sufficiently marinated (after $\frac{1}{4}$–$\frac{1}{2}$ hour), a quantity of boiling broth is poured onto the food to provide it with just the right amount of final cooking.

(e) *Sui Bāo* or 'Water Sizzling' is much the same process as the previous method, except water is used instead of broth in the final steeping.

In both of the last two cases the dishes produced might be called 'semi-soups'. They are not strictly soups because they are eaten more for their ingredients than for the soup itself.

2. *Shuān* can best be described as 'Quick Plunging'. This takes place in boiling broth and is usually done at the dining table, where a charcoal-heated hot-pot keeps the broth at a rolling boil. The materials to be cooked (beef, lamb, chicken) are sliced into razor-thin slices and then plunged into the boiling broth to cook for no more than $1-1\frac{1}{2}$ minutes. They are then retrieved and dipped into sauces or mixes (the dry seasonings) before eating.

3. *Liu* is a double-heating process of cooking which can probably be best described as 'Wet Quick-Fry'. The raw material – very often fish – is first of all cut into thin bite-sized pieces. It is then lightly battered with egg white and cornflour, plunged into boiling water or hot oil for about a minute and drained.

In a frying pan a mixture, usually consisting of 1 or 2 teaspoons of chopped ginger and onion, is stir-fried with a couple of table-spoons of oil. Into this is added salt, sugar, broth, sherry (or white wine), gourmet powder and cornflour (blended in a small amount of water). When the sauce thickens the sliced fish is added and turned over gently in the sauce, with slight addition of clarified lard or sesame oil, for $\frac{1}{2}-1$ minute or so, before serving. (Where available wine-sediment paste is used instead of sherry.)

4. *Kuo Yih* can probably best be described as 'Marinated and Dry-Braised'. The food to be cooked, most often fillet of meat or breast of poultry, is usually cut into reasonably thin slices. These are then marinated in finely-chopped onion, ginger, wine, salt, gourmet powder for 15–20 minutes before being battered, dredging lightly in flour first and then dipping in beaten egg. They are then fried in a small amount of oil. The food should be laid in a single layer in the pan, and the latter should be tilted and shaken over

moderate heat to ensure even heating. When both sides have been fried, a few tablespoons of chicken broth is added to the pan. The tilting and shaking of the pan is continued until all the liquid has dried up, when the food will be ready to serve.

5. *Kao* is roasting, which is by no means a common method, since ovens are seldom seen in Chinese kitchens. In Peking it is done by hanging the food to be cooked in a brick oven over a charcoal fire. Peking Duck is a well-known dish cooked in this manner.

6. *Tieh* or *Kuo Tieh* is a form of static frying where a minimal amount of oil is used; during the period of cooking the top of the food is sprinkled now and then with water, broth, or vinegar mixed with water and broth. This sprinkling helps the top part to stay moist, soft and tender, while the bottom part is fried to a crispness. Thus you can achieve a double quality (softness and crispiness) in one mouthful of food. A typical dish cooked in this manner is Kuo Tieh, a form of Chinese ravioli, which is steamed first and fried last.

7. *Kan Shāo* is very similar to Kuo Yih (method 4), The only difference is that the food to be cooked is neither dipped in batter nor marinated before cooking. All the seasonings, flavouring materials and main ingredients are added during the frying. In the last phase of the cooking, a small quantity (4–6 tablespoons) of chicken broth and wine is added. The food is ready as soon as the liquid has evaporated. Giant prawns are often cooked in this manner.

Often when meat is cooked in this manner, a small amount of lard (1 tablespoon) or sesame oil (2 teaspoons) is added immediately after the liquid in the pan has dried up for a final stir-fry. At the same time the food in the pan is sprinkled with a spoonful of chopped coriander or chives. This method is sometimes also known as deep-fried and cooked.

8. *Lou*. To 'lou' is to cook food in a quantity of 'master sauce', which consists, apart from water, mainly of soya sauce and sugar, small amounts of tangerine peel, anise star, ginger and salt and an

even smaller amount of five-spice powder. As more meats are cooked in this 'sauce' it becomes more and more enriched. It can be kept 'alive' indefinitely by replenishing the herbal ingredients after every third or fourth time it is used. Meat, fish and fowl, apart from being enriched in colour, become slightly 'aromated' when cooked in it.

The 'Aromated and Crispy' dishes are meats which have been cooked in the 'master sauce' and then deep-fried to crispiness just before serving.

9. *Por.* To 'por' is to deep-boil. This is another method of cooking which Peking has inherited from Chinese Moslem cooking which flourished over the great plains of Mongolia and Singkiang. As cattle are often slaughtered and cooked whole or nearly whole in these frontier areas, a great deal of material and water are involved in the cooking. What Peking cooking has learnt from this style is that if a great quantity of meat is deep-boiled in water not all the flavour will be dispersed into the soup. Indeed much of the flavour will return into the meat, and this can be seasoned, flavoured and regulated. Hence in this type of cooking, meat is often simmered for 5–6 hours or more. When required, the meat, which has now achieved complete tenderness, is quickly deep-fried and dipped in sauce for eating, or it is briefly cooked with a few fresh seasonings and flavouring materials in an earthen casserole and served.

10. *Sha Kuo* or 'Earthen-pot casserole cooking'. Casserole cooking in China is generally a lengthy process of simmering over a low charcoal fire. But in Peking, as already intimated under the previous method of 'Por', it can be quite a rapid process where a slowly-cooked main material is further cooked in a casserole or earthen-pot together with wine, a few flavourings and seasoning ingredients for a mere 15–25 minutes. Because it is easy to achieve many permutations of seasoning and flavours, a large number of casserole dishes can be created in this manner.

11. *Kao Li* is cooking food wrapped in a layer of egg white which has been beaten until stiff. This method is often used for a sweet called Kao Li To Sha which is sweetened bean paste balls, wrapped

in a thick layer of mixture of beaten egg white and cornflour and then deep-fried.

12. *Fu-Yung*. Egg white is used extensively in Peking cooking, usually in the form of a white sauce in which beaten egg white is mixed together with minced chicken, cornflour, broth and seasonings. Everything becomes 'fu-yung' when this white sauce is added or cooked with it. The 'fu-yung' is sometimes not used with anything but is cooked and eaten on its own. In the Peking Fu-Yung Sliced Chicken, the 'fu-yung' mixture is not applied to pieces of chicken, but the mixture itself, which contains some minced chicken and minced white fish, is floated on hot oil and forms smooth white slices which resemble chicken breasts. This is what Fu-Yung Chicken Slices are.

13. *Pa-SSi*. Pa-Ssi in Chinese means 'drawn-thread', which describes the very thin thread which results when molten glass or thick syrup is drawn out. In favourite forms of Peking desserts – such as Drawn-Thread Apple – the fruit, in bite-sized pieces, is given a turn in hot syrup of molten sugar, and then immediately plunged into ice-cold water to become brittle and glazed. When the pieces of fruit are pulled apart or taken out of the containing bowl, they draw behind them a long thread. Hence the name of this particular form of treatment.

14. *Liu Hu*. This is another form of cooking which is peculiar to Peking. It consists of scorching the meat either over a barbecue or under the grill before subjecting it to other forms of cooking. This initial scorching until the meat is slightly burnt has the effect of giving the meat a smoky flavour.

15. *Bāo Hu* can be translated as 'Scorched-Frying'. It consists of heating food – often marinated meat and onion – on a dry metal surface. This can be the surface of an ungreased frying pan or a griddle, but it must be a large flat area. The food to be cooked should be turned over from one unused part of the heated surface to another until it is slightly burnt. Again it is the controlled scorching which gives it the smoky flavour which is demanded by the connoisseurs of Peking.

PART TWO

Principal Restaurants in Peking and Some of their Best-Known Dishes

CHAPTER ONE

The Chinese Moslem School

Many of the best-known and most impressive dishes of Peking are the produce of this school of cooking, such as Barbecued Meats, Sliced Lamb Hot Pot, Earthen-Pot Casserole of Pork, Scorched-Cooked Pork, Cooked Deep-Fried Pork, Scorched-Fried Beef (or Lamb), Cooked Whole Lamb, Peking Duck (roasted) and its various subsidiary dishes.

I shall try in this chapter to make it possible for the reader to savour these and other dishes of the Peking restaurants where they were best-known; and to provide cooking instructions for them, in so far as it is practicable in normal Western households to reproduce these dishes to approximate to their originals. The names of some of the restaurants should arouse pleasurable nostalgia in the hearts of all Peking exiles and those who have ever indulged themselves in Peking.

BARBECUED MEATS OF BARBECUE WAN
AND BARBECUE CHI

烤肉宛　　　　烤肉季

Barbecued meats were first introduced in Peking towards the end of the Ming Dynasty. During the reign of Emperor Sung Chi (1644–1661) there were many visits from the princes and dignitaries of Mongolia, who were all keen on eating beef and lamb. During those early days, cooked meats sprinkled with water were used for the barbecues; these were eaten with spring onions or leeks, dipped in soya sauce. Fresh raw lamb or beef began to be

43

used only sixty or seventy years ago. There are now many establishments in Peking which serve these barbecued meats. The two best-known are the Barbecue Wan and the Barbecue Chi.

Barbecue Wan has been in continuous trade for six generations, more than 200 years. It is situated in the southern part of the city, along Sung Nu High Street. Barbecue Chi has been established for over a century, and lies in the north of the city, outside the Ti-An Men Gate beside a creek called Cha Liu Stream. Because of its cool situation, it carries on its business even in the heat of the summer, when most of the other establishments are closed. The two establishments were simply and commonly known as 'Wan of the South' and 'Chi of the North'. Their methods of preparing their famous Barbecued Meats were as follows:

Equipment

In Peking, meat barbecues are cooked on a large basin-shaped open brazier, which is placed on a rough table. The brazier is topped with a two-foot diameter wire-meshed range, with spaces of approximately a quarter of an inch in between the wires. The brazier is in turn placed on top of a round iron tray, filled with a layer of earth, to prevent the heat of the brazier from burning the table top. The normal fuel used is charcoal made from the cypress tree, the willow, or the pine and pine kernels. The latter types are considered the best.

Meat

The meat used can either be beef or lamb. But the beef must come from animals which have not been doing heavy labour; or, if they have, it must not have been for too long a period before slaughter. As far as a lamb is concerned, the particular animal must weigh about 50 lbs (those of 40 lbs are considered too thin, and those of 60–70 lbs too fat).

Only the fillet, sirloin, rib and rump of beef are used; and the leg, saddle and shoulder of lamb. The meat has to be hung for five or six hours in a breezy place in order to reduce its natural water content. When that has been done, it would be wrapped and placed in a refrigerator overnight before slicing.

Slicing
When the meat has been chilled overnight it is ready for slicing. It is sliced on a chopping board against the grain in strips about 2″ wide and 5–6″ long. Several pieces of meat can be placed one on top of another, wrapped in a piece of cloth with only one end protruding, and sliced simultaneously. The knife used has a crescent-shaped blade with a straight back and is approximately 15–16″ long. Working at a steady pace, an experienced cutter can slice a dozen to fifteen pieces in a minute. The pieces should be smooth and of an even thickness (rough $\frac{1}{8}$″) without any signs of sawing.

Firing and Testing
The charcoal in the brazier should be fired about 15–20 minutes before the commencement of the barbecue, and the wire-meshed range should first be rubbed with a piece of beef or lamb fat. After a while, test the range with a drop of water. If the drop sizzles and evaporates quickly the brazier is ready for use.

Barbecuing and Eating
Before the barbecue starts, see that each person is provided with a bowl in which he will mix his own concocted sauce, made from the following selection of basic ingredients: soya sauce, shrimp sauce, dry sherry, ketchup and ginger water (simmer 1 tablespoon of sliced root ginger in 6 tablespoons of water for 3 minutes). In addition he should be given a supply of very thinly-sliced spring onions (scallion) which have been tied into shoe-lace or lover's knots.

When all is ready, place a 'knot' of onion on top of the range to grill, and then dip a piece of meat in the prepared sauce-mixture and place it on top of the onion. Turn the meat over a few times in the course of the grilling which should last about 1–$1\frac{1}{2}$ minutes. During the last part of the grilling, a pinch of coriander leaves may be added to the meat or, if that is unavailable, a pinch of watercress or parsley.

When the meat is done, it is lifted onto the diner's plate and eaten with a toasted Peking Hot Cake (see page 68). In the West, the hot bun that is eaten with hamburgers can be used. The meat, coriander and onion can all be wrapped or sandwiched inside the 'cake'. For added piquancy and crunchiness, raw cucumber strips, some plum sauce and soya jam may also be added. The Peking Hot Cake is more aromatic than a hamburger bun as it is studded with sesame seeds.

About $\frac{1}{2}$–1lb of meat is normally allowed for each person. The ideal number at a barbecue like this is between four and eight persons.

SCORCHED-FRIED MEATS OF THE MOSLEM DINING ROOM

回民食堂

Meats cooked in this manner are one of the very few items of food which have been introduced into Peking from Manchuria. They have a history in Peking of no more than 70–80 years. Originally they were a type of instant cooked meat plied and sold by street-vendors who pushed a kind of two-wheeled barrow with a small coal-burning stove on it, together with other wares and equipment required for their trade. People would gather around the cart just as people gather around a small bonfire, or a hot hamburger stand on a cold winter's day. It was only latterly that meat cooked in this manner has become adopted as restaurant food. It is now sold with great success by the Moslem Dining Room, which is situated just outside the Chien Men Gate.

These scorched-fried meats are, in fact, not fried at all in the conventional sense. Ordinarily meats are fried in oil–in this case no oil is used. Here they are heated or scorched on a dry pan, after being brushed with sauces and flavouring ingredients. The pan has to be very large and flat, and the meat should be sliced against the grain into pieces 3–4″ long, $1\frac{1}{2}$″ wide, $\frac{1}{6}$″ thick. The pan or flat metal surface should be hot enough for the slices of meat to sizzle when they are placed on it.

The meats generally used for such cooking are beef and lamb;

and the flavouring ingredients used to brush on it are: soya sauce, chopped ginger in vinegar, shrimp sauce, sesame oil. A large pinch of shredded onion is placed on the pan to heat at the same time as the meat.

The important point to bear in mind when using this method is that the meat must be cooked quickly (if it is to retain its tenderness) and at the same time the outside of the meat must become slightly scorched. To achieve this the pan has to be very hot and well heated before anything is placed on it. When the meat appears to be cooked on one side (about one minute) it should be turned over and cooked on the other, on a different spot of the pan. It is then turned over quickly 6–7 times, each time onto a new spot. Being in contact with hot dry metal the surface of the meat will have become slightly scorched after 3–4 minutes, when the meat will be ready to serve. The degree of 'scorchedness' can be varied according to taste. It is the slight burn on the surface of the meat which gives it its smoked effect and special flavour.

Meat prepared in this manner is eaten with onions, in conjunction with Hot Cakes or toasted buns.

TRIPLE-COOKED MUTTON OF PAI KWEI MOSLEM RESTAURANT OF LUNG FU SU (LUNG FU TEMPLE), PEKING EAST

隆福寺白魁燒羊肉

This establishment was first founded in the forty-fifth year of the Reign of Emperor Chien Lung, and has been in continuous trade for nearly 190 years. It was founded by a person called Pai Kwei, who was eventually banished to Singkiang for telling risqué stories in the Palace. The business was inherited by his chief chef, Ching Fu, whose family ran it for four generations.

It eventually went into the hands of the Hei family. After Liberation with a view to preserving the Chinese culinary heritage, a member of the Ching Family, Ching Shiao Shan, who had inherited the true technique of the food preparations, was restored to run the kitchen of the restaurant.

The technique practised at the Pai Kwei Moslem Restaurant in preparing its mutton is to cook the whole lamb, together with its head, neck, tail, heart, liver, lung, kidney, etc.—altogether fifteen separate items—in one large pot. The following is a summary of the operation:

Preparation
Prepare a large cauldron of a 'master sauce' by heating together 1 cwt of water with a quantity of yellow bean paste and black bean paste, together with appropriate amount of salt. After bringing to boil and 20 minutes' simmering, filter the liquid through muslin into several large bucket-containers for use.

Cooking
Heat 50 lbs of the resultant 'sauce' in a large cauldron. When it starts to boil place pieces of lamb meat (cut into 6–7 lb sized chunks) into the cauldron to boil for 15–20 minutes. They should be put in, one piece after another, only when the liquid in the cauldron starts again to boil fully. When all the pieces of meat have been 'tightened' (as the term is) they are forked out and put aside.

Meanwhile treat all the different parts of the lamb similarly. When this part of the process is completed the used sauce is poured away and replaced by a fresh quantity of sauce. Into this second sauce are added various flavouring and herbal ingredients, such as tangerine peel, anise stars, crystal sugar, onion, garlic, dried mushrooms, chopped ginger, parsley, tarragon, etc. (up to a total of 24 types of herbal and flavouring ingredients can be added). When this has been done the pieces of lamb are added into the cauldron one after another, the toughest pieces at the bottom and the more tender pieces on top. The walls of the cauldron are lined inside with pieces of heart, lung, liver, kidney, legs, tail etc., and the whole build-up is finally crowned with the lamb's head on the very top. A round pan or basin containing 25 lbs of water is then used to press down all the meat from the top. The contents of the cauldron are then brought to a rapid boil for 30 minutes. It is during the end of this period that the herbal and flavouring ingredients are adjusted.

48

During the next phase of the cooking, which is continued in the same cauldron, 3 pints of strong mushroom water (simmer $\frac{1}{2}$ lb dried mushroom in $3\frac{1}{2}$ pints water for 30 minutes) are added into the soup. Continue now to heat the contents of the cauldron at a merest gentle simmer for the next 3 hours (keeping the meat under weight).

Serving
When this phase of the cooking is completed, the pieces of lamb are forked out and placed to drain grouped according to different parts of the lamb.

When the pieces are well-drained, those which are to be eaten are then placed in a separate pan to deep-fry in sesame oil for 7–8 minutes, whereupon they are ready to be served.

These long-cooked fried-meats are usually eaten (they should be so tender by then that they could be broken into smaller pieces by a pair of chopsticks) with Hot Cakes (or toasted buns), and washed down with Yellow Wine (or Shiao Shing wine, dry sherry of dry white wine); or they can be added to half a bowl of cooked noodles, into which is poured half a bowl of the rich broth or soup derived from the 3 hours of long-simmering the lamb, sprinkled liberally with vinegar and freshly ground pepper.

⌄ If this recipe is tried in an average Western kitchen, the scale of things will, of course, have to be reduced. All the same you should not cook with less than 6–7 lbs of lamb. The cooking can be done in a large deep casserole in the oven at 300 degrees (Regulo 1) for 3 hours, after the initial period of boiling. The main flavouring ingredients, such as Chinese dried mushrooms and bean pastes are normally obtainable from Chinese provision stores, and the herbal ingredients can be made up by using a couple of bags of bouquet garni. The final frying of the pieces of lamb intended for immediate eating should be done, properly speaking, in a fondue dish or in an electrically heated pan on the table, so that the diners may feel the benefit of the heat, which is a part of the flavour of the dish.

LAMB HOT-POT OF TUNG LAI SHUN

東來順

Tung Lai Shun is situated in the East Market of Peking, described in the Introduction. It was originally just a food vendor's open stall and the best-known place for this style of Lamb Hot-Pot was then at the famous Sheng Yang-Lou, which had established business over one hundred years before. However, Tung Lai Shun, which only started in 1903, managed in 1913 to obtain the chef as well as several of his assistants from the more established restaurant. It has since gone on from strength to strength, and now employs over one hundred people, of whom twenty odd are expert meat slicers of high metropolitan repute. These men can keep up a pace of 12–15 pieces (size $7'' \times 2'' \times \frac{1}{6}''-\frac{1}{5}''$ thick) a minute. For this particular dish the lamb meat has to be sliced fresh whenever it is required. It should not be sliced first and left for any length of time.

Equipment

The Peking version of the hot-pot used for this dish was partly developed at Tung Lai Shun. It is a charcoal-burning funnelled hot-pot; the contents of the pot are contained in a moat surrounding a fat, squat-based funnel at the centre into which the hot charcoal is packed. This funnel rises 4 inches above the lid of the pot (which is left on only before the soup in the moat comes to the boil). Its overall length is about a foot, but it can sometimes be lengthened by slotting in an additional funnel-attachment on top to provide the extra draw. In any case the firing-power of the pot is impressive and is able to keep the soup and other materials in the moat (which holds some 3–4 pints of liquid) at a constant rolling boil.

Other Materials

Unlike other styles of hot-pots in China where a dozen different types of foods can be packed into the pot to cook together, the ingredients used, beside the lamb, in the Peking Hot-Pot are very simple; they consist of no more than spinach, or Chinese cabbage, (about $\frac{1}{2}$ lb to be added in 4 different lots at 4 different times),

¼ lb transparent noodles (also to be added in 4 different lots), and 4–5 pints of bone-broth (starting with 3 pints, adding the rest as you go along).

For Dipping and Additional Flavouring
Coriander leaves, vinegar, shrimp sauce, sesame jam, chilli oil, mashed bean-curd cheese, soya sauce. Each diner can concoct his own sauce-mixture from these ingredients as he pleases in a bowl provided specially for him for this purpose.

Sliced Lamb
Pieces of sliced lamb are laid out in sheets of one layer on some four to six medium-sized plates. The diner picks up a piece or two at a time with his chopsticks and dips and cooks it in the broth boiling in the moat of the hot-pot. These pieces of lamb do not require much more than $1\frac{1}{2}$–2 minutes of cooking, after which they are retrieved by the diner, dipped lightly in his own 'dip-bowl' and eaten. The dipping appears to have two functions: to enable the food to pick up additional piquancy and to give it a chance to cool somewhat before insertion into the mouth.

Lamb cooked in this manner can be eaten on its own, without any supporting rice, cakes or toasted buns. In fact, once started one has the feeling that one can go on eating forever. In between mouthfuls of meat, one eats a spoonful or two of soup and spinach or cabbage, with a few strands of transparent noodles. As there is so little fat and so few carbohydrates, this dish might indeed prove an ideal dieting formula (or feast) for those bent on reducing. All the time as one cooks the soup becomes more and more tasty. In the end, each person fills his own bowl to give it all a last 'wash down', which brings beads of perspiration to everyone's forehead–a particularly fit conclusion to a hearty meal in the chill of winter.

If you are cooking Lamb Hot-Pot in the West, use a fondue dish, or electrically heated pan on the table. The calculation should be $\frac{3}{4}$–1 lb of lamb per person. The hot-pot itself is sometimes available in Chinese provision shops and the Chinese ingredients required are always available in such stores.

THE PEKING DUCK OF CHÜAN CHÜ TE'
AND PIEN I FANG

全聚德　　　便意坊

The two best-known places for Peking Duck in Peking are Chüan Chü Te' (established in 1864), and Pien I Fang (established in 1855). Both restaurants specialise in this internationally famous dish. With roughly a century's experience behind each of the establishments their expertise is unchallenged. Their aim is to produce a roast duck with a crackling aromatic skin and the tenderest meat, which is rich in taste, appealing in its creamy colour and yet without the slightest suggestion of being greasy. It is these qualities which enable this duck to be eaten repeatedly and always with undiminished pleasure and appreciation.

The Duck

The most important factor in this dish is, of course, the duck itself. The bird used in Peking Duck is a local produce, specially reared for the dish. It is also reared in Inner Mongolia, Cheng Te' and Tientsin. It has since been introduced to England and America (in 1875), to Japan (in 1888), and to the Soviet Union only in 1956.

This duck has feathers of pure white and a slight tip of yellow on its beak. It has short wings as well as short legs, with a long broad back, giving an appearance of sturdiness. In contrast with other species of duck which often have dark, dry flesh, the flesh of the Peking duck has fine streaks of white fat embedded in its pinky-cream lean flesh. When roasted the meat is a degree richer than that of the average duck. According to a book published in 1956 by the Chung Hua Publishing Co., entitled *The Rearing of Peking Duck* (by Wu Tze), the duck requires no more than 3 months rearing before being ready for the oven. During the last 30 days it is artificially fed twice a day. In that time a drake will reach 7–8 lbs and a duck 5–6 lbs.

The Oven

The next important thing in the preparation of Peking Duck is the oven, which is not often found in Chinese homes, or even in the average restaurant. Hence the dish can normally be eaten only in specialised restaurants.

At Chüan Chü Te' the oven is built like a kiln, rectangle outside and round inside. The ducks to be roasted are hung on iron rods with wooden handles. Just below where they hang, and somewhat behind where the charcoal burns is an inclined piece of sheet-iron, which catches the dripping and conducts it along a short gutter. This gutter leads through the brickwork outside into a bucket provided for the dripping. Ducks roasted in such an oven are called Hung-Roast Duck which is the orthodox way in which Peking Ducks are cooked (in contrast to other ways in which they can be roasted).

Preparation

After the duck has been plucked and thoroughly cleaned, it is inflated by pumping air with a foot-pedal pump between the windpipe and the skin. The rubber tubing should be inserted an inch or two into the neck, along and beside the windpipe, and both tubing and windpipe gripped firmly together outside the neck with the left hand. When pumping has inflated the bird about 70–80 per cent, the right hand should be used to press the back of the bird forward against the neck. The result of this pressure is that the bird becomes more completely inflated and the skin loosens from the body. Pumping should then continue for half a minute or more. From then on, the bird should be handled only by the neck, wings, legs or tail, not by the inflated body. After the tubing is withdrawn, the neck is tied up.

The skin of the duck is then doused with boiling water and thoroughly dried. The duck is then hung up to dry in an airy spot, for 4–5 hours in the summer and overnight in the winter.

Before roasting, the skin of the duck is rubbed with sugar water (approximately 1 part of malt sugar to 6 parts of water) and allowed a short further period to dry. Then the duck is ready for roasting.

Roasting

In the very large oven used in the restaurant, a small duck of 3–3½ lbs requires no more than 30 minutes to cook; and even large birds of 5–6 lbs would require no more than 45–50 minutes. Any part of the duck which is not quite brown to liking can be subjected to a short period of grilling.

Slicing and Eating

When the duck is ready the slicing of the skin and meat is usually done with the right hand with a peeling action. The skin of the duck is peeled off first and served on one plate, and then the meat is peeled off and placed on two or three other serving plates or dishes. When this is being done, the duck should be on a wooden block which is in turn placed on a metal dish (pewter) so that any excess oil or liquid which flows from the carcass will flow away from the body and will not affect the crispiness of the crackling skin.

When eating, the crackling skin and delicious tender meat of the duck are arranged lengthwise on a doily that is as thin as a pancake, but smaller in size (see page 55); some pieces of crunchy raw vegetables, such as segments of spring onion and sliced cucumber, are added. Then they are brushed with some piquant sauces and ingredients, such as plum sauce, bean paste, jam, chopped garlic in vinegar, etc., and rolled up altogether into a roll which is eaten with the fingers. It is probably the combination of all the different crackling, rich, crunchy and piquant qualities in one roll which makes Peking Duck so memorable.

The carcass of the duck is often cooked with cabbage and made into a soup, which is used to round off the meal–for after a further series of rich elaborate dishes, it is usually concluded with a selection of deliberately plain and simple ones, including the soup.

If cooked in the West, Peking Duck, which in England appears to be the Aylesbury Duck, can be roasted in an oven at 400 degrees (Regulo 6) for precisely 1 hour. It should be first of all doused with a kettleful of boiling water, dried and hung overnight. The sugar water used to rub on the duck can be made with 1 part barley or malt sugar to 6 parts of water. The oven need not be opened at all (the duck should not be basted) during the hour in which it is being roasted. The skin of the duck cooked in this fashion can be very crispy. It is important that it should be eaten rolled in a pancake or doily as in Peking, if the quality of the dish is to be apparent.

PANCAKES OR DOILIES FOR PEKING DUCK
½ lb. flour; 4/5 of a cup boiling water; 2 tablespoons sesame oil

Preparation
Sift flour into a large basin. Add boiling water gradually. Mix with spoon into a dough. Knead dough for 6–7 minutes, and allow to stand for 10 minutes.

Make dough into a long roll about 2″ diameter and cut it into $\frac{1}{2}$″ thick discs. Use knife to pat and flatten dough discs into pieces of about 3″ diameter. Brush the tops of two pieces of dough discs with sesame oil, place one piece on top of the other, the greased surfaces facing each other. Use a rolling pin to roll the double pieces of dough (from centre out and on both sides) into approximately 6″ diameter pancakes.

Cooking
Heat an ungreased heavy frying pan over moderate heat. When hot place a piece of double-pancake to heat on the ungreased surface for approximately 3 minutes on either side, when spots of brown should appear and parts of the pancake will start to bubble.

Remove the pancake from the pan, and when slightly cooler pull each double-pancake apart into two. The greased sides should detach themselves without difficulty. Fold each pancake or doily across the centre on the greased side.

When all the pancakes have been heated and folded, stack them on a heatproof dish, and steam them for 10 minutes, when they should be ready. These pancakes or doilies can be kept in a refrigerator for several days, but will require several minutes of vigorous steaming (7–8 minutes) before serving.

CHAPTER TWO

From the Palace Kitchen

During the latter part of the Manchu Dynasty (1644–1911) the memoirs of whose last Emperor Pu-Yi were quoted in the Introduction – there were the following kitchens in the Palace:

The Kitchen of Longevity, the Tea and Snack Kitchen, the Kitchen for the Emperor's Routine Meals, the Kitchen of the Princes and Royal Concubines, the Mobile Picnic and Travels Kitchen. These were in turn divided into:

The Meat Kitchen, the Vegetable and Vegetarian Kitchen, the Rice Kitchen, the Pastry and Snacks Kitchen, the Barbecue, Roasting and Preserves Kitchen. They employed a total of about 300 chefs, cooks and assistants.

FANG SHAN RESTAURANT OF NORTH SEA PARK

仿膳(清宫風味)

The first restaurant in Peking to prepare food in the style of the Palace was established in the Pai Hai Park (North Sea Park) in 1925 by a person called Yueh Ren Chi who engaged a number of former Imperial cooks and chefs to prepare Palace dishes. The establishment later went through several hands until, in 1955, the People's Republic nationalised it, bringing it under the Peking Parks and Forest Bureau.

Under the new management, it was successful in inviting and recalling several ex-Imperial chefs from their retirement, among them, in 1956, Ngiu Wen Chi (aged 69), Yang Ching San (aged

74), Wen Pao Tien (aged 70), Wang Yu San (aged 73) and Pang Wen Hsiang (aged 74).

What is surprising is that many of the dishes which originated in such a complex outfit are comparatively simple, although there are some which are highly elaborate (many of which can now be produced in a modern kitchen in a matter of minutes however).

Minced Pork Stir-Fried with Green Peas

½ lb lean pork; ½ lb fresh green peas (or frozen); ½ teaspoon salt; 1 tablespoon chopped onion; 1 teaspoon chopped fresh ginger; ½ tablespoon soya sauce; 1 tablespoon soya-bean paste; 3 table- spoons good broth; 2 tablespoons dry sherry; ½ chicken stock cube (or ½ teaspoon gourmet powder); ½ tablespoon cornflour (blended in 2 tablespoons broth); 2 tablespoons lard; 1 teaspoon sesame oil.

Preparation
Chop pork into a rough-grained mince. Pour boiling water over the green peas in a bowl, leave to stand for 1 minute and then drain.

Cooking
Heat lard in a frying pan. When it has all melted add the pork, sprinkle with salt and stir-fry over high heat for 2 minutes, until the meat has lost all its pinkness. Add the onion, ginger and bean paste. Continue to stir-fry over moderate heat for 1 more minute. Add the peas, stock cube (broken), soya sauce, sherry, broth. Stir-fry for a further 2 minutes.

Finally, add the cornflour mixture and sesame oil, turn up the heat and stir-fry for ½ minute and serve.

This was quite a regular dish served in the Palace during the spring and summer seasons when the peas were sweet and fresh. Although the preparation and cooking are comparatively simple, it is highly appetising.

Minced Pork Stir-Fried with Diced Cucumber

Repeat the preceding recipe and substitute ½ lb of cucumber for green peas. The cucumber should be diced after slightly scraping its skin, not peeling it. Unlike peas it does not need to be soaked in boiling water. It can be added into the pan to stir-fry immediately after dicing.

This is another favourite dish which was served frequently in the Palace during the spring and summer.

Empress Dowager's Square-Cut Pork Pudding

2 lbs belly of pork; 2 pints Master Sauce (see below); 1 cup chicken broth; 2 tablespoons soya sauce; 1 tablespoon chopped onion; 1 teaspoon chopped ginger; 1 teaspoon sugar; 2 tablespoons dry sherry; ½ tablespoon cornflour (blended with 2 tablespoons chicken broth).

FOR MASTER SAUCE

2 pints water; 2 bags (or sacs) bouquet garni; 2 tablespoons dried tangerine peel; ½ tablespoon anise star; 6 tablespoons sugar; 1 cup soya sauce.

Preparation

Prepare the Master Sauce by bringing to boil and simmering all its ingredients together for half an hour.

Cooking

Boil the belly of pork in water for half an hour. Transfer it to the Master Sauce to simmer for 15–20 minutes until it is quite brown.

Drain the meat, when cool place it on a chopping board and cut it through the skin into four square pieces. Now use a pointed sharp knife and carefully cut through the skin three concentric squares one smaller than the other right through each piece of pork; the line of the cut should in fact be continuous. By entering the pork on one of the sides the knife takes a right angle turn each time it nears the next side. By so doing the knife gradually moves toward the centre in straight lines parallel to the sides. It does this by making a smaller square each time a square is about to be completed so that a shape like a squared-off concentric spiral results. When each piece of pork is cut in this manner it is placed in a bowl, skin-side downwards. When all four pieces are in the bowl sprinkle them with chicken broth, soya sauce, chopped onion and ginger, sugar and sherry. Place in a steamer and steam for three-quarters of an hour.

When ready turn the pork out on a well-heated deep-sided dish. Pour the gravy into a small pan. Add the cornflour blended with chicken broth. Stir over high heat until the gravy thickens (in 15 seconds). Pour the gravy over the pork and serve.

This used to be one of the dishes served on the Empress Dowager's birthday.

The Big Casserole (also called 'Quadruple of Tenderness')

2–3 lbs chicken; 2½ lbs pork (lean); ½ lb dried seaweed (the type that yields iodine); 2 lbs bamboo shoots; ½ lb onion; ½ lb leeks; 4 cloves crushed garlic; ¼ pint soya sauce; ¼ lb sugar; ¼ pint vinegar; ½ pint dry sherry; 4 tablespoons sesame oil; 2 lbs pork bones; 6–8 pints water.

From the quantities of the above materials and ingredients, which are already much reduced from the original recipe, it is obvious that a very large casserole or iron pot, with 4–5 gallon capacity, would be required to cook this dish. Within the confines and limitations of the modern household, it might be necessary to reduce the quantities of all the ingredients by half except for the chicken. Such a reduction should not very materially affect the outcome of this dish. In this case it should be possible to cook it in a very large iron casserole in the oven at 400 degrees (Regulo 6) for half an hour and 300 degrees (Regulo 1) for a further 3½ hours.

Preparation
Chop both the chicken and the pork into 1½" pieces. Cook the chicken in boiling water for 2½ minutes and pork for 5 minutes and drain.

Soak the dried seaweed in water for 1 hour. Clean thoroughly. Simmer in boiling water in a copper pan for half an hour. Drain and slice into $1\frac{1}{2}''$ squares.

Give the bamboo shoots a blow or two with the side of the chopper (to loosen their texture). Cut them into strips $1\frac{1}{2}''$ long and $\frac{1}{2}''$ wide. Simmer in boiling water for 3 minutes and drain.

Skin and cut each onion into 6–8 slices, leeks into $1\frac{1}{2}''$ long segments.

Arrange the pork bones at the bottom of the iron pot or casserole. Arrange the pork, seaweed, chicken, bamboo shoots, leeks and onion in layers, one on top of the other. Finally sprinkle the packed ingredients with garlic, sugar, soya sauce, vinegar, sherry and sesame oil. Now pour in sufficient water to cover all the solids by half an inch.

Cooking

After bringing the contents to boil reduce heat to a minimum (and insert an asbestos sheet under the pot, if an iron pot is used) and simmer for $3\frac{1}{2}$ hours. Whether cooked in a casserole or an iron pot, the original container used should be brought to the table.

This is one of the favourite dishes served in the Palace in the winter. It is said to have the distinction of possessing the characteristics of sweetness, sourness, richness and tenderness all at once, besides being extremely digestible. The presence of a large quantity of sugar can probably be attributed to the Empress Dowager, who was well known for her sweet tooth.

Lotus Leaf Wrapped Pork

$1\frac{1}{2}$ lb belly of pork; 3–4 large pieces of lotus leaves (if dried, soak to soften); $\frac{1}{4}$ lb rice; 1 tablespoon sugar; 2 tablespoons soya sauce; $1\frac{1}{2}$ tablespoons soya paste; 1 tablespoon chopped onion; 1 teaspoon chopped ginger; 1 clove garlic (crushed); 1 tablespoon dry sherry.

Preparation

Stir-fry the rice gently in a dry pan for 8–10 minutes over low heat, until the rice has turned brown. Pour it on a board and roll it with a rolling pin into breadcrumb-sized grains (and use it as a kind of aromatic breadcrumbs).

Cut the pork through the skin into pieces 2″ long, 1″ wide and ½″ thick.

Mix the sugar, soya sauce, soya paste, sherry, onion, ginger, garlic in a bowl. Turn the pork in the mixture until each piece is well and truly covered. Leave it there to soak for 15 minutes.

Meanwhile, soak and clean the lotus leaves (if fresh) in hot water for 5 minutes and cut into 3″ × 4½″ sheets. Take a piece of marinated pork, roll it in roasted ground rice and wrap it in a sheet of lotus leaf. Wrap it in envelope fashion and tuck the tongue in firmly. Pile the wrapped pieces of pork to the one side (tucked-in side downwards–place a weight on top if necessary to keep the wrapping in place) while the rest of the pork is being wrapped and parcelled.

Cooking
Arrange all the wrapped parcels of pork in a fireproof dish. Place it in a steamer and steam for 1½ hours.

When serving bring the fireproof dish to the table; each 'parcel' of pork is opened by the diner with a pair of chopsticks during the meal.

This was one of the favourite dishes served in the Palace during July and August when lotus leaves are plentiful and the flowers in full blossom in the lotus ponds. Pork cooked in such a manner carries with it the scent of the lotus leaf and the aroma of roasted rice, along with its usual richness of taste and flavour.

Scrambled Bean Curd (Originally called 'Bean-Curd Brain' or 'Sweetmeat')

¾ lb bean curd; 4 large Chinese dried mushrooms; 3 teaspoons cornflour (blended with 3 tablespoons chicken broth); 2 tablespoons lard; 3 teaspoons melted chicken fat; 2 teaspoons soya sauce; 1 teaspoon salt; 1 tablespoon chopped onion; ½ teaspoon chopped ginger; ½ teaspoon gourmet powder; 6 tablespoons chicken stock; 2 tablespoons sherry.

Preparation

Soak mushrooms in warm water for 1 hour. De-stem and slice into matchstick strips.

Cut each bean curd into 10–12 pieces.

Cooking

Heat lard in a frying pan. When it has melted add the onions, ginger and mushrooms. Stir-fry them together over high heat for 1½ minutes. Add the bean curd. Use a metal spoon or spatula to mash and mix the bean curds with the other ingredients. Add salt, soya sauce, gourmet powder, sherry and chicken stock. Continue to stir-fry vigorously for 2½ minutes. Add blended cornflour mixture and chicken fat. Stir-fry for another half minute and serve.

This was one of the favourite dishes of the Empress Dowager during her old age and last years on the throne. It is extremely delicate, dissolving in the mouth almost as one eats, with the fried mushroom and onions each contributing its own flavour.

Fried and Steamed Pork and Crab Balls

½ *lb crab meat (lightly cooked or canned); 4 tablespoons finely chopped pork (fat and lean); 4 tablespoons finely chopped potatoes; 2 eggs; 1 tablespoon cornflour; ½ teaspoon salt; 1 tablespoon finely chopped onion; 2 thin slices ginger; 2 tablespoons chicken broth; 2 tablespoons finely chopped ham; 1 tablespoon finely chopped chives; oil for deep-frying.*

FOR SAUCE:

3 *teaspoons cornflour (blended in 2 tablespoons water); ½ cup chicken broth; salt to taste; pepper to taste; ½ teaspoon gourmet powder (or Ac'cent); 2 teaspoons chicken fat; 1 tablespoon sherry.*

Preparation

Mix the crab meat, pork, potato, eggs, cornflour, salt, onion and ginger in a basin until they become a thoroughly blended paste.

Cooking

Heat oil in the deep-fryer over moderate heat for 5 minutes. Take a handful of crab-pork paste, and squeeze it through the hole made by rounding your index finger, into small $\frac{3}{4}''$ diameter balls. Scoop the balls with a tablespoon, and drop them into the boiling oil to deep-fry. Use up all the paste and deep-fry each of the balls for approximately $3\frac{1}{2}$ minutes, when they should start to turn brown.

Remove the balls from the deep-fryer to drain briefly. Then place them in a shallow fireproof dish. Sprinkle with 2 tablespoons chicken broth, place the dish in a steamer and steam for 20 minutes.

Meanwhile blend the cornflour and chicken broth together for the sauce. Add salt, pepper, gourmet powder, chicken fat and sherry. Heat them together in a small saucepan. Stir until the sauce thickens.

When the crab-pork balls are ready, remove from the steamer, pour the sauce over them. Sprinkle them with chopped chives and ham and serve.

In Peking this is usually a summer dish when crabs are plentiful.

Triple Quick-fry

$\frac{3}{4}$ *lb lamb; $\frac{1}{2}$ lb lamb liver; $\frac{1}{2}$ lb lamb kidney; 3 stalks spring onion; 3 tablespoons soya sauce; 3 tablespoons dry sherry; $1\frac{1}{2}$ tablespoons cornflour; pepper to taste; $1\frac{1}{2}$ tablespoons vinegar; 1 clove garlic (chopped); 2 teaspoons mustard powder; 2 tablespoons sesame oil; 2 tablespoons vegetable oil.*

Preparation

Slice lamb, liver and kidney separately into pieces roughly $2\frac{1}{2}''$ long and $1''$ wide. Add soya sauce, sherry and pepper to each. Sprinkle with cornflour, working it in with the fingers.

Cut spring onion into $1''$ segments.

Cooking

Heat oil in a *large* frying pan over moderate heat. Add lamb, liver, kidney pieces and fry them in different parts of the pan for 2 minutes and push them to the sides. Add sesame oil, spring onion, garlic, mustard and vinegar into the centre of the pan, stir them together. Turn up the heat to the highest. Turn, toss and scramble the meat, liver and kidney together with all the fresh ingredients for half a minute. Serve piping hot.

Braised Bamboo Shoots

1 lb dried bamboo shoots; 1 slice root ginger (chopped); 1 tablespoon chopped spring onion; 2 tablespoons soya sauce; 6 tablespoons chicken broth; 2 tablespoons dry sherry; 1 teaspoon gourmet powder; 2 teaspoons sugar; 1½ tablespoons lard; vegetable oil for deep-frying.

Preparation
Soak dried bamboo shoots in warm water for 1 hour. Drain and cut into segments 2½″ long and ½″ wide.

Cooking
Heat vegetable oil in a deep-fryer. Deep-fry the bamboo shoots for 2½ minutes. Remove and drain.

Add lard to a frying pan. When hot, stir-fry the onion and ginger in it for ¼ minute. Add soya sauce, broth, sherry, sugar and gourmet powder. Stir and add all the bamboo shoots. Turn them in the sauce until each piece is well covered.

Reduce heat to low and allow the bamboo shoots to simmer for 10–12 minutes (until quite dry) and serve.

One of the attractions of this dish to the Chinese is its crunchiness. It is said to have been introduced into the Palace menus during the reign of Chein Lung (1736–1795).

Stir-Fried Diced Chicken with Shrimps

½ lb breast of chicken; ¾ lb shelled shrimps (fresh or frozen); 3″ segment of cucumber; 1 teaspoon salt; 1 tablespoon cornflour;

2 tablespoons chopped spring onion; 2 teaspoons chopped root ginger; 3 tablespoons dry sherry; 2 tablespoons soya sauce (light colour); 2 teaspoons sugar; 3 tablespoons vegetable oil; 2 teaspoons sesame oil.

Preparation
Dice chicken and cucumber separately into $\frac{1}{3}''$ cubes. Sprinkle both chicken and shrimp with salt and then cornflour, working it in with the fingers.

Cooking
Heat 2 tablespoons vegetable oil in a large frying pan. When hot add chicken and stir-fry over moderate heat for $\frac{1}{2}$ minute and set aside. Add remaining vegetable oil and shrimps. Stir-fry for $1\frac{1}{2}$ minutes. Add sesame oil to centre of pan and all the other ingredients. Turn the heat high, continue to stir-fry for one more minute and serve piping hot.

Sliced Fish Fillet in Sour and Sweet Sauce

$\frac{2}{3}$ lb fillet of fish (sole, halibut, carp, bream, etc); 2 tablespoons cornflour; 1 tablespoon finely chopped onion; 1 teaspoon finely chopped root ginger; oil for deep-frying; 2 tablespoons lard.

FOR SAUCE
$1\frac{1}{2}$ tablespoons soya sauce; 2 tablespoons vinegar; 2 teaspoons sugar; 2 tablespoons sherry; 3 tablespoons chicken broth; 3 teaspoons cornflour (blended in 2 tablespoons water).

Preparation
Slice fish with a sharp knife into pieces 2″ long, 1″ wide and $\frac{1}{4}''$ thick. Sprinkle and rub the pieces evenly with cornflour.

Mix all the ingredients for sauce in a bowl until they are well-blended.

Cooking

Heat oil in the deep-fryer until very hot. Lower the pieces of fish into the oil one by one. Deep-fry them for approximately 2 minutes. Remove and drain.

Heat lard in a frying pan. When it has all melted add the onion and ginger to stir-fry over high heat for $\frac{1}{2}$ minute. Reduce heat to moderate. Pour in the sauce mixture. Stir until it thickens and becomes translucent. Add the slices of fish carefully into the sauce, spreading them out over the pan. With the help of a fish-slice turn the pieces of fish a couple of times over in the sauce.

Transfer the pieces of fish onto a well-heated serving dish. Pour the remaining sauce in the pan over the fish. Serve piping hot.

Deep-Fried Crackling Pork 'Sandwich'

$\frac{1}{2}$ lb fillet of pork; 6 slices (3″ × 4″) very thin ($\frac{1}{8}$″ thick) sheet pork fat; 3 teaspoons cornflour; 3 tablespoons flour; 1 egg; 2 tablespoons water; 1 tablespoon finely chopped onion; 1 teaspoon finely chopped root ginger; $\frac{1}{2}$ teaspoon salt; 1 tablespoon soya sauce; pepper to taste; 1 tablespoon sherry; oil for deep-frying.

Preparation

Slice pork into pieces approximately $1\frac{1}{2}$″ long and 1″ wide. Place them in a bowl and add onion, ginger, salt, soya sauce, pepper and sherry. Mix pork well with seasonings to marinate for 10 minutes.

Beat flour, cornflour, water and egg in another bowl into a batter.

Divide the sliced pork into 3 equal portions after turning them in the batter. Place or spread several pieces of sliced pork in between two sheets of pork fat and form them into a 'sandwich'. Press them together on a flat surface so that they will flatten and stick together. Continue till three 'sandwiches' are made.

Cooking

Heat the oil in the deep-fryer until very hot. Lower the 'sandwiches' into the oil one by one to fry over high heat for 2 minutes. Reduce the heat to low and continue to fry for another 3 minutes. Turn up the heat again to the full for the final 1½ minutes' frying. By this time the sandwiches should have turned brown and fat become crackling. Remove the pork 'sandwiches' from the hot oil and drain.

Chop each 'sandwich' into 4 and serve on a well-heated serving dish. To be eaten dipped in salt and pepper mix (blend 1 tablespoon salt with 1 teaspoon freshly milled pepper and heat them on a dry pan over moderate heat for ¾ minute).

This is an unusual dish with both crackling and meaty qualities.

Dry-Fried Minced Pork

The Palace style Dry-Fried Minced Pork is unusual in that it is fried without any oil at all. Nor are any supplementary materials (such as vegetables, etc.) used. The only things added are various seasonings (ginger and garlic being in this case regarded merely as seasonings). The purpose here is to produce a dish of finely-chopped meat, which is extremely light and verges on a velvety crispiness.

1½ lb leg of pork; 1 tablespoon brown bean paste; ½ tablespoon soya sauce; 2 teaspoons sugar; 1 teaspoon finely chopped root ginger; 1 clove garlic (crushed and finely chopped); 2 tablespoons dry sherry; 1 teaspoon sesame oil.

Preparation
Chop the pork with a pair of choppers into approximately rice-grain sized pieces (coarse mince).

Cooking
Heat a large frying pan over high heat. Add the minced pork, spread it over the pan to stir-fry for 2 minutes. Scrape the pan quickly to prevent sticking. Reduce the heat to low and continue to stir-fry for another 2 minutes. Increase the heat to high and

stir-fry again for ½ minute, scraping continually to prevent sticking. Then stir-fry over low heat for 1½ minutes. Repeat this sequence 2–3 times when quantities of oil will have started to sweat and flow from the meat. Tilt the pan, and press the meat with a metal spoon. Pour as much of the oil away as possible. Transfer the meat to another dry pan, which is placed over moderate heat. Add bean paste, soya sauce, sugar and stir-fry, scramble and scrape for 2 minutes.

Then add ginger, garlic and sherry. Continue to stir-fry, scramble the meat and scrape the pan. As soon as all the liquid has dried up, reduce to low heat and continue to scrape and stir-fry until the meat appears light, dehydrated and crispy. Finally sprinkle the meat with sesame oil, continue to stir-fry for 1 minute and serve.

The idea of this off-and-on heating (or frying) is to bring the meat to the verge of being scorched and then save it by the reduction of heat and by stirring. When the process is repeated a number of times the meat should become progressively lighter and dehydrated and more aromatic and crispy.

Pork prepared in this special way is excellent with rice, or on sesame-sprinkled 'Hot Cakes'.

The Peking Hot Cake

The Peking Hot Cake is really an unleavened bread, with the slight addition of sugar and sesame oil and made aromatic by its layer of roasted sesame seeds. In Peking special utensils and stoves are used to make them. As we have seen it is eaten with an extensive range of meat dishes.

1¼ lb flour; 1 teaspoon baking powder; 3 teaspoons sugar; ½ pint water; 1 tablespoon sesame oil; ½ teaspoon salt; ¼ lb sesame seeds.

Mix sugar and flour and baking powder in a basin. Add water gradually, mix with a wooden spoon. Sprinkle the sesame oil evenly over the dough. Mix and knead well. Roll and form the dough into a long 1″ diameter roll. Cut the roll into 1½″ long segments and form each segment into a ball. Roll or flatten the balls into crumpet-sized flat cakes. Moisten one side of the cake with water and press this damp side down on the sesame seeds which have been spread out on a flat tray so that the cakes take on a layer of seeds. Place them in one layer on a dry flat pan over moderate heat for 4–5 minutes, seed side up, until the bottoms are beginning to brown. Then place them, seed side up, to toast under a moderate grill for 3–4 minutes, or until brown, when the cakes will be ready. They go well with most meat dishes.

Steamed Rolls (or Hua Chuan, 'Flower Rolls')

This is another item which is eaten with various meat dishes, whether dry-fried, crispy-roasted, braised or stewed in casseroles: with crispy and dry-fried meat, the soft absorbent texture of the rolls sets off the meat's dry-crispiness; with the braised and casserole dishes, the spongy quality of the rolls helps to soak up the gravy.

1¼ lb flour; 1½ teaspoons baking powder; ½ pint water; 1 tablespoon sugar; 1 tablespoon sesame oil; 1 teaspoon salt.

Preparation
Mix flour, baking powder and sugar together in a bowl, adding the water gradually. Mix and knead well. Let the dough stand for a couple of hours to rise.

Divide the dough into two parts. Roll each into a flat sheet about 18″ long, 8″ wide and ⅛–⅕″ thick. Brush one surface of each of the sheets with sesame oil and sprinkle with salt. Roll one sheet inside the other (the oiled side against the unoiled) into an 18″ long roll. Cut roll into 2½″ segments and as it is cut, press the centre of each segment with a pair of chopsticks, so that the ends open up like flowers.

Cooking
Place the segments or rolls on a cloth-covered surface in the

steamer to steam vigorously for 15–17 minutes. Suitable for eating with most meat dishes especially those with plentiful sauce or gravy.

Cold Soya Pork

3–4 lbs hand or knuckle of pork; 2 pints soya sauce; 2 tablespoons sugar; $\frac{1}{2}$ teaspoon Five-Spice powder; 2 teaspoons chilli sauce; 2 envelopes or packets of bouquet garni.

Preparation
Simmer pork in boiling water for 10 minutes, remove bone (cut it out). Place pork meat in a large glass or earthen container and add all the marinating ingredients. Turn pork over every half hour for the first 3 hours, thereafter once every 12 hours. Leave the pork to season and marinate for *three days*.

Cooking
Drain the pork of its marinade (which can be used again for other purposes). Place it in a fireproof dish, and steam vigorously for 1 hour 40 minutes. Remove from steamer and allow it to cool. When cold slice the meat into thin pieces, 2″ long and $1\frac{1}{2}$″ wide and serve. Excellent for an hors d'oeuvre.

Chilled Spiced Chicken

3 pairs pork trotters; 3 pints water; 2 medium onions; 2 slices root ginger; 1 chicken ($2\frac{1}{2}$–3 lbs); 2 teaspoons salt; $1\frac{1}{2}$ pints water; 1 carrot; 2 stalks spring onion (in 2″ segments); 4 table-spoons sherry; pepper to taste.

Preparation
Chop onion into quarters. Boil and simmer gently with trotters and ginger in 3 pints water for 2 hours, which should reduce liquid to nearly half. Skim away oil and impurities. Strain liquid into a casserole or heavy pan.

Quarter chicken and further chop through bone into 16–20 pieces. Scrape and cut carrot into triangular wedges.

Cooking
Heat chopped chicken in 1½ pints water, adding salt and carrot. Simmer for half an hour. Skim away impurities and pour away half of the top layer of the water.

Add the chicken and carrot to the pork trotter stock. Add sherry, spring onion and pepper. Simmer gently for half an hour. Pour the contents into a large fireproof dish or fireproof glass basin. Allow to cool and place in refrigerator to chill for 2–3 hours. Serve by turning the chicken and jelly out onto a large serving dish. The chicken in jelly can be set off more attractively by arranging a bouquet of colourful vegetables or even flowers (such as lettuce, tomatoes, chrysanthemums) around it.

Pheasant Hot-Pot

There are a good many universal hot-pots in China, but this one is definitely a regional dish. It came to Peking from Manchuria with the Manchus in the 16–17th century. Apparently pheasants flourished in the pine forests of Manchuria.

1 *pheasant (2–3 lbs); 2 cakes bean curd (each piece cut into 8); 3 tablespoons soya sauce; 1 teaspoon chilli sauce; 1 tablespoon shrimp sauce; 2 teaspoons sesame paste; 2 stalks spring onion (1″–segments); 3 tablespoons pine kernels; 3 tablespoons chopped salted Chinese pickled greens ('Red in Snow'); 1 pint chicken broth; 1½ pints water.*

Preparation
Boil the pheasant for 15 minutes. Let it cool and bone it with a sharp knife. Cut its meat into slices approximately 1½″ long and 1″ wide.

Heat broth and water in a pan. Add pine kernels and pickled greens to simmer for 20 minutes. Pour the contents of the pan into the moat of the hot-pot (see Lamb Hot-Pot, page 50) and stoke up the charcoal heat so that it blazes.

Cooking
Bring the hot-pot to the table. Add bean curd, soya sauce, shrimp sauce, chilli sauce, sesame paste, onion and finally sliced pheasant. Place the hot-pot at the centre of a round dining table and allow the contents to simmer for 20–25 minutes. Then the lid of the pot can be taken off and the diners help themselves to the contents, both with their spoons as well as their chopsticks.

PORK DISHES OF SHA KUO CHÜ OR 'HOME OF THE EARTHEN-POT CASSEROLE'

沙鍋居

The restaurant of Sha Kuo Chü was founded in the Sixth Year of the Reign of Emperor Chien Lung (1741). During all its history of more than two hundred years it has used an enormous earthen-pot of 4 ft. diameter for the basic cooking of its pork dishes. The establishment was originally called Ho Sung Chü ('Home of the Smooth and Peaceful') but because of its impressive casserole it came to be known as Sha Kuo Chü ('Home of the Earthen-Pot Casserole').

It was first started in one of the outhouses of the Imperial Palace. As the story goes, it originated from the Dawn and Dusk Sacrifices practised during the Ching Dynasty, as well as the Sun and Moon Sacrifices, when a first-class whole pig was slaughtered. When the sacrifices were over the carcasses were removed to the outhouses. There the court attendants in co-operation with Imperial Kitchen staffs proceeded to develop three types of dishes: the 'White-Cooked' dishes, the 'Deep-Fried' dishes, and the 'Scorched-Cooked' dishes. At first, only the more humble members of the household were interested in these dishes. But gradually they gained adherents even amongst the senior members of the Imperial Court, as well as interest from the public at large.

However, the supply of raw material was limited to only one sacrificial pig a time. Hence the place was open for business only until noon, when everything was 'cleaned out'. Indeed, it was not until 1937 that the convention was altered. More materials were purchased, and Sha Kuo Chü was open for business all day.

White-Cooked Pork

'White Cooking' is the basic culinary method employed by Sha Kuo Chü. It involves cooking quantities of pork meat by simmering it in ample water over a low fire for a long time. The pig's heart, lungs, intestines, tripe and liver are similarly treated to separate lengthy cooking.

In the preparation of White-Cooked Pork, all the pig can be used except the head, trotters and heels. Cut the meat into strips of about 6″ long and 3–4″ wide. Then place all the pieces in a huge casserole and add water to cover by 3″. Bring the contents to the boil, and reduce the heat to a minimum–just enough to maintain a slight simmering. The important thing is that no water whatever should be added in the course of cooking which should last 2 to $2\frac{1}{2}$ hours depending on the toughness of the pork (or even 3 hours if the pig is exceptionally old). The casserole should be covered, and grease and oil skimmed off the surface of the water or soup every $\frac{1}{2}$–$\frac{3}{4}$ hour (after the initial skimming which should take place 10 minutes after it first boils).

When the pork is ready lift the pieces out of the casserole, and remove the skin and bones. When the meat is slightly cooled, slice the pieces into *thin* 3″ × 4″ sized pieces, and serve.

Pork cooked in this way should be eaten with 'steamed buns' or with Peking Sesame Hot Cakes (as with the Barbecued Meats). A sauce mixture is added, made up by the individual diner from the following ingredients: chopped garlic, segments of spring onion, soya sauce, sesame oil, chilli oil, mashed Southern bean-curd cheese.

73

If attempted in the West, the pork is best cooked in a deep old-fashioned iron pot, using a minimum of 6–7 lbs of meat. It can either be simmered over a low fire, or placed in an oven at 300 degrees (Regulo 1) for $2\frac{1}{2}$–3 hours, after it has first been brought to the boil. It should be eaten with toasted hamburger buns together with the same sauces. The ingredients can be purchased from Chinese provision shops.

The special qualities of pork cooked in this way arise from its long simmering, since (a) all heaviness and greasiness disappear, (b) it is extremely tender and tasty (the latter can be achieved only if a large quantity of pork is cooked), (c) the lean parts are in no way fibrous, dry or wood-like, as overcooked meat often turns out to be (this is possible because of the extremely low-heat cooking). Consequently in a Western kitchen, if the pork is not cooked in the oven but on the range, an asbestos sheet should be placed between the flame and the iron pot.

White-Cooked Lung, Liver, Tripe, Intestines, Heart

The second series of dishes produced at the Sha Kuo Chü is made from the pig's heart, liver, lung, tripe and intestines, which are cooked in the same manner as the pork. I shall not go into great detail about their preparation, as they are not usually eaten in the average Western household, but the material used should be very thoroughly cleaned and soaked for alternate periods in brine and vinegar.

When they are cooked together, the lungs should be put into the pot first, followed by the tripe, then the intestines, the heart and finally the liver. After the initial boiling and simmering, the liver is cooked and removed first (30 minutes), the heart next (1 hour), followed by the intestines ($1\frac{1}{2}$ hours), then the tripe (2 hours) and finally the lungs ($2\frac{1}{2}$ hours). All these are sliced and served on separate plates, and can be eaten along with the White-Cooked Pork, using the same sauce mixtures, together with toasted buns or Hot Cakes.

The Small Casserole Dishes

The third series of dishes at Sha Kuo Chü is prepared from the products of the first two series.

The white-cooked meat or other white-cooked items are placed in a small casserole (approximately 6″ in diameter and 3″ deep) with the addition of:

> 1 tablespoon chopped onion; 1 slice root ginger; 1 teaspoon salt; 4 tablespoons dry sherry; ½ teaspoon gourmet powder (or ½ chicken stock cube); ¼ lb Chinese white cabbage (or spinach, celery); 4 tablespoons of thinly sliced bamboo shoots; 4 tablespoons of soaked Chinese dried mushrooms (de-stemmed).

The correct method of cooking is to place the cabbage (or spinach or celery) at the bottom of a small casserole. Cover it with ¾ lb of sliced white-cooked pork (or ½ lb of the liver, lung etc.,) and spread or sprinkle the other items and ingredients on top of the pork. Add the rich stock derived from the original cooking of the pork to fill three-quarters of the casserole.

Cover, bring the contents to the boil, and simmer gently for 20 minutes. Serve by bringing the casserole to the table. The dish, accompanied by a little rice, is a great favourite of the Pekingese. It combines the richness of the soup and the melting-tenderness of the pork, together with the freshness of the vegetables.

Deep-Fried Pork Dishes

The fourth series of dishes produced at Sha Kuo Chü is produced in two ways:

Deep-Fried Pork Fillet Rolls

Slice white-cooked fillet of pork into pieces 3″ long, 1¼″ wide and ⅕–¼″ thick. These are then individually wrapped in a slightly larger sheet of pork-suet seasoned with a small amount of chopped onion, root ginger and salt.

When the pork has been rolled in the suet the latter is secured by tying it in two places with string or a firm dried stringy vegetable. When a sufficient number of these rolls are made, cook them for 15 minutes in boiling water, drain and then deep-fry them in hot oil for 2 minutes until they are beginning to turn brown. Whereupon remove from oil, drain, slice into $\frac{1}{5}$–$\frac{1}{4}''$ slices and serve.

Deep-Fried Stuffed Intestines (called 'Deer's Tail')

1 lb minced white-cooked pork (fat and lean); $\frac{3}{4}$ lb liver; 4 tablespoons minced pine kernels; 1 tablespoon chopped onion; 1 teaspoon chopped ginger.

Mix them all together into a stuffing. Stuff a length of well-cleaned intestine with this mixture. Tie up both ends of the intestine firmly with string, and also all along the length at 3″ intervals. Lower this length of 'sausage' into a pan of boiling water to boil for 20 minutes. Then lift it out, prick a tiny hole in each segment and return to boil for another 10 minutes. Finally remove the string and deep-fry the sausage in hot oil for $2\frac{1}{2}$–3 minutes until brown. Slice each segment into four and serve.

Both the Deep-Fried Pork Fillet Rolls and the Stuffed Intestines should be eaten dipped in aromated salt-pepper mixture (heat 1 tablespoon salt with 1 teaspoon freshly milled pepper on a dry pan for $\frac{1}{2}$–1 minute).

The Scorched-Cooked Dishes

These dishes consist of scorching the meat by grilling or barbecuing it (often the head or the end pieces: the trotters and heels) until the outside is scorched and slightly burnt. The important thing is that the scorching and burning should be done evenly (this can be best done in a modern kitchen on a rotisserie under high heat). When the piece has been 'scorched' immerse it in water for half an hour. Drain it and brush it with a very stiff brush to remove any really burnt bits. When this has been done rinse it and then boil or simmer it slowly for about 2–2½ hours in the same manner as White-Cooked Pork was. The slightly burnt taste gives it an unique smoky flavour, which many Pekingese find appealing. Although the head and the end pieces are often cooked in this way, it is the 'knuckle of pork' (back leg) or the 'hand of pork' (front leg) which are considered the best pieces for the purpose.

When ready the meat is sliced very thin and eaten with the same sauce-ingredients and Hot Cake (or toasted hamburger buns) as with White-Cooked Pork.

Sesame Pork Balls

The Sha Kuo Chü has quite a number of pork dishes. This one I felt worth mentioning because of its unusualness. It consists of mincing ½ lb pork (lean and fat), and mixing or blending it with 3–4 tablespoons of cornflour. Form the mixture into approximately ½″-diameter balls. Deep-fry these balls in oil for 2½–3 minutes until they are browned.

Meanwhile heat 3 tablespoons sugar in a separate pan with 2 tablespoons of oil. Heat over moderate heat for 2 minutes (not more as it might over-caramelise). Add the pork balls and turn them in this hot syrup. As soon as they are well covered with this molten sugar, pour them onto a large flat plate spread with a layer of sesame seeds (slightly roasted). Allow the pork balls, covered with molten sugar, to pick up the seeds, until they are completely covered with this additional aromatic layer. Allow a little time to elapse for the sugar to cool and become brittle, when the dish will be ready to serve.

According to the Pekingese, the crackling sweetness on the outside and the soft meatiness on the inside of the meat-balls, together with the aromatic effect of the sesame, all join to make the creation an intriguing dish.

CHAPTER THREE

Hopei and Shangtung Styles of Cooking

Hopei and Shangtung are the two adjacent North China provinces which bestride the lower Yellow River and border on the Gulf of Chili. It is probably natural that their cuisine forms more or less the basic indigenous cooking of Peking. For Peking is after all situated in Hopei; and since Shangtung is its immediate neighbour to the south, as well as being the cradle of Confucian culture, the two provinces can almost be regarded as one. Geographically Hopei, which borders on Manchuria on the east and Inner Mongolia on the north, is a couple of hundred miles further north and therefore more subjected to the seasonal winds from Siberia. The air there is a fraction drier and the land more arid than in Shangtung; the climate a fraction more severe. The eastern part of Shangtung is a peninsula which juts out into the North China Sea. The coasts and ports on both the north and south sides of the peninsula are ideal for summer holidays—the sun hot, water warm and fruits plentiful. In both provinces, there are wide plains and fertile soil. An abundance of agricultural produce is reflected both in the markets as well as the culinary practices of this region. Compared with the south, strong vegetables such as garlic, ginger, onions, leeks and spring onions (scallions), and sesame oil and seeds are much more universally used.

CHUI HUA L'OU ('PAVILION OF ASSEMBLED LUXURIANCE')

萃華樓

Chui Hua L'ou was first established in 1940. Situated in Pa Mien Cho Broadway, it is one of the largest of the Shangtung-style restaurants in the city; with time it has achieved a considerable reputation. Its chef, Chu Yu Kung, was chosen to run the Chinese Kitchen at the Moscow Chinese Agricultural Exhibition in 1953, where his reputation was further enhanced.

The following are some of the dishes prepared by him and his associates:

Quick-Fried Diced Chicken in Bean Paste

½ lb breast of chicken; 1 egg white; 1 tablespoon cornflour; 1½ tablespoon water; 2½ tablespoons brown bean paste; 1½ teaspoons sugar (brown, fine grain); 1 teaspoon finely chopped ginger; 1½ tablespoons dry sherry; 2 tablespoons vegetable oil; 2 tablespoons lard.

Preparation
Dice chicken into ⅓″ cubes. Blend cornflour with water. When well mixed, add egg white and beat together with a pair of chop-sticks (or fork) for ½ minute. Add chicken to the blended egg white and cornflour batter, and mix well.

Cooking
Heat oil in a frying pan. When hot add the diced chicken. Stir-fry for 1¼ minutes. Remove and drain, and pour away all the oil.

Add lard to the frying pan. When it has all melted add the brown bean paste and stir it into the lard. When most of the moisture in the paste has evaporated and the sizzling noise has reduced, add the sugar, ginger and sherry. Stir them together for 12–15 seconds. Return the chicken to the pan. Stir and mix them

79

together with the bean paste for 15–20 seconds, dish out and serve to be eaten piping hot.

Sliced Fish in Wine Sauce

$\frac{1}{2}$ *lb fillet of fish (sole, bream, mullet, halibut); 1 egg white; 2 tablespoons water; 1 tablespoon cornflour; 2 tablespoons 'wood-ear' fungi (clean and soak in water for half an hour); oil for deep-frying.*

FOR SAUCE

4 tablespoons white wine; 4 tablespoons chicken broth (concentrated); $\frac{3}{4}$ tablespoon cornflour (blended with 3 tablespoons water); 1 teaspoon finely chopped ginger; 2 teaspoons finely chopped onion; $\frac{1}{2}$ teaspoon sugar; $\frac{1}{2}$ teaspoon salt; $\frac{1}{2}$ teaspoon gourmet powder; 2 tablespoons lard.

Preparation

Clean and slice fish into pieces $1\frac{1}{2}''$ long, $1''$ wide and $\frac{1}{5}''$ thick.

Beat egg white, water and cornflour into a batter. Add batter to fish and mix well. Steep the 'wood-ear' fungi in boiling water for 2 minutes and drain.

Cooking

Heat oil in the deep-fryer. Spread half the slices of fish in wire-basket. When the oil is very hot, fry the fish pieces in it for 30 seconds and remove to drain. Continue till all the fish is cooked.

Heat lard in a frying pan. Add onion and ginger to stir-fry for $\frac{1}{2}$ minute. Pour in the chicken broth and add the sugar, salt and gourmet powder. Lay the fish onto the broth piece by piece, spread evenly over the pan. When the contents start to boil pour in (or sprinkle) wine evenly over the fish. Tilt the pan so that the sauce will flow over the pieces of the fish. Then add the blended cornflour, pouring it evenly over the pan. Turn the pieces of fish with a small fish-slice (or pair of chopsticks). Heat for another $\frac{1}{4}$ minute.

Arrange the 'wood-ear' fungi neatly around the sides of a dish and pour the fish and sauce in the centre.

This recipe is distinguished by its contrast: the white of the fish and the ample winey translucence of its sauce setting off the black of the fungi, which also provide a complete contrast in texture with their slippery crunchiness.

Plain Fried Fish in Wine Sauce

1 whole fish (carp, trout or bream, approximately 1½ lbs); 2 tablespoons flour; 2 eggs; 1½ teaspoons salt; 6 tablespoons lard.

FOR SAUCE
2 stalks spring onion (1" segments); 1 tablespoon brown bean paste; 2 teaspoons sugar; ½ teaspoon gourmet powder; 1 tablespoon soya sauce; 4 tablespoons sherry; 2 teaspoons brandy; 1 clove garlic (chopped).

Preparation
After cleaning the fish thoroughly and drying, score or slash the sides of the fish at 2" intervals (each cut approximately 1½" long ¼" deep). Rub the fish with salt and flour and leave to stand for half an hour. Beat eggs with a rotary beater for 10–15 seconds. Moisten the fish thoroughly with the beaten egg.

Mix all the ingredients for sauce in a bowl, blend well.

Cooking
Heat lard in a large frying pan. When it has melted lower the fish into the pan to fry over high heat for 15 seconds on either side.

Reduce heat to low, allow the fish to fry for 10 minutes on either side, basting now and then. Pour away all excess fat. Turn the heat up high. Pour the sauce mixture over the fish in the pan. Tilt and move the pan so that the fish will be thoroughly covered with the sauce. Then turn it over with the help of a fish-slice. Continue to cook over high heat for 1 minute and serve on a well-heated oval dish.

The dish has a strong aromatic appeal, and the colour of the fish is rich, golden brown.

FENG TSE YUAN ('GARDEN OF ABUNDANT BENEFIT')

豐澤園

The Feng Tse Yuan is a well-known Tsinan-style restaurant (Tsinan is the capital of Shangtung). It was established in 1930 just outside Tsien Men in Mei Ssi Street, and is famous for its soups and lightly-cooked dishes.

Sliced Duck's Liver Soup

10 *oz duck's liver; 1½ pints superior chicken broth; 1 teaspoon sugar; 1 teaspoon salt; 1 teaspoon gourmet powder; 2 slices root ginger; 3 teaspoons chicken fat; 2 tablespoons chopped parsley.*

FOR THICK WINE SAUCE
1 *tablespoon brown bean paste; 1 tablespoon tomato puree; 1 tablespoon soya sauce; 1 teaspoon sugar; 1 tablespoon finely chopped onion; 1 teaspoon finely chopped ginger; 8 tablespoons dry sherry; 1 tablespoon brandy.*

Preparation
Prepare the thick wine sauce by simmering the first seven ingredients for the sauce together in a heavy pan, stirring occasionally with a wooden spoon, until the volume has been reduced by half. Allow the liquid to stand overnight. Add the brandy. Stir and strain through muslin into a jug.

Soak liver in fresh water for 2 hours. Drain and slice into $\frac{1}{6}''$ thick slices. Immerse the sliced liver in boiling water for a minute and drain.

Cooking
Heat chicken broth in a saucepan. Add salt, sugar, ginger, gourmet powder and thick wine sauce. When it boils, skim away any impurities. Add all the liver. When the contents reboil, sprinkle

the soup with chicken fat and parlsey and serve in a large soup bowl.

Hot and Sour Fish Soup

1lb fillet of fish (sole, bream, carp, halibut, salmon, etc); 1 egg white; 1½ tablespoons cornflour (blended in 2 tablespoons water); 2 pints superior chicken broth; 2 tablespoons thinly sliced onion; 1 slice root ginger; 1 teaspoon salt; 1 teaspoon gourmet powder; 1 tablespoon sherry; ¼ teaspoon black pepper (or to taste); 4 tablespoons vinegar; 2 stalks spring onion (chopped); 1 tablespoon chopped coriander; 1 teaspoon sesame oil; 1 tablespoon lard; oil for deep-frying.

Preparation

Slice fish into thin pieces, 1½″ long and 1″ wide. Beat egg white and cornflour together with a rotary beater for 20 seconds. Turn the sliced fish in the batter so that each piece is evenly covered.

Cooking

Divide the fish slices in two lots and deep-fry them in hot oil for 1½ minutes each. Drain.

Heat lard in a large saucepan. Add ginger and onion to stir-fry for ¾ minute. Pour in the chicken broth. When latter boils, add fish, salt, sherry, gourmet powder, pepper. Bring to boil and simmer gently for 10 minutes. Sprinkle with vinegar, coriander, spring onion and sesame oil and serve in a large tureen or soup bowl.

Soft-Hearted Prawn Balls

8 oz prawn or shrimp meat; 2 tablespoons pork fat; 3 tablespoons cornflour; 3 tablespoons mashed potato; 2 eggs; ¾ teaspoon salt; 1 tablespoon dry sherry; 6 tablespoons meat jelly; oil for deep-frying.

Preparation

Chop prawn and pork fat with a pair of choppers into a fine mince.

Mix them with cornflour, mashed potato, beaten egg, salt and sherry. Blend them well together with a beater and form the mixture into 12 to 15 balls.

Meat Jelly: if this item is not readily available it can be made as follows: boil $\frac{1}{4}$ lb pork skin, 1 pair of pork trotters and $\frac{1}{2}$ lb lean pork together for 10 minutes. Pour away the water and place all ingredients in a casserole. Add 1 pint water, 1 slice root ginger, 2 tablespoons soya sauce, 1 tablespoon sugar and 3 tablespoons sherry. Place it in an oven and heat under cover for 15 minutes at 400 degrees (Regulo 6) and $1\frac{3}{4}$ hours at 300 degrees (Regulo 1). Then remove and pour all the fluid from it into a basin. Put the basin in a refrigerator to allow the gravy to jellify, which it should do, into a firm 'meat jelly', in $2\frac{1}{2}$–3 hours. Scrape away any congealed fat on top of the jelly. Spoon out a few spoonfuls and cut into small pieces for use.

Make a deep dent or hole in each of the prawn-balls. Insert a piece of meat jelly into the hole. Close and cover over the hole with additional prawn–potato–egg mixture and roll again into round balls.

Heat oil in the deep-fryer. When hot, place half the prawn balls in a wire basket and lower them to deep-fry for $2\frac{1}{2}$ minutes over moderate heat. Remove and drain and repeat with the second half of the prawn balls. When both lots of prawn balls have been fried once and drained, heat the oil in the deep-fryer over high heat and return all the balls for a final frying for $1\frac{1}{2}$–2 minutes, or until the balls are golden brown.

These prawn-balls should be eaten dipped in salt-and-pepper mix. They are intriguing because of the liquid heart of molten meat jelly. But do not be in a hurry to bite into them as the gravy can be quite hot. Bite lightly.

Casserole of Tripe

1 lb pork tripe; 1 pint superior chicken broth; 2 slices root ginger; 3 tablespoons thinly sliced onion; 2 tablespoons soya sauce; 1 teaspoon salt; 3 tablespoons dry sherry; 1 teaspoon gourmet

*powder; pepper (to taste); 2 tablespoons chopped coriander;
2 teaspoons chicken fat.*

Preparation

Simmer tripe in water for 2 hours. Drain and slice with a sharp knife into thin strips (twice matchstick thickness). Return the tripe into a fresh pan of boiling water to boil for 5 minutes and drain.

Cooking

Heat chicken broth in a saucepan. When it boils add tripe, salt, soya sauce, sherry, ginger, pepper, onion, gourmet powder. Reduce heat and allow them to simmer for 15 minutes. Sprinkle with chicken fat and coriander and serve in a tureen or large soup bowl.

The purpose of this recipe, as with the other soup recipe from the Feng Tse Yuan, is not to produce a highly savoury soup (which is easy enough in Chinese cooking), but something light, plain and fresh in flavour. It is these soups which are often the most appreciated when the table is otherwise packed with savoury dishes during a Chinese banquet or dinner party.

CHÜAN CHÜ TE' ('RESTAURANT OF COMPLETE AMALGAM OF VIRTUES')

全聚德

Chüan Chü Te' is another Shangtung-style restaurant situated outside Chien Men at Number 24, the 'Meat Market' (Jou Ssi) where it started business in 1864. We have already mentioned its Peking Duck which is internationally famous. This establishment has a branch at Number 80, West Chang an Chieh ('Boulevard of Eternal Peace') which is well-known for its other duck dishes, as well as for a good range of Shangtung dishes.

Chopped Boiled Duck in Mustard and Thick Wine Sauce

½ *boiled duck (cold–having been boiled for* 35 *minutes only);* 3 *tablespoons 'thick wine sauce' (preparation as in Duck's Liver Soup page:* 82); 2 *teaspoons powdered mustard;* 1½ *teaspoons soya sauce;* 3 *teaspoons vinegar;* 1 *teaspoon sugar;* 2 *teaspoons sesame oil.*

Preparation
Chop the duck with a sharp cleaver (Chinese chopper) on a heavy chopping board into a dozen bite-sized pieces. Arrange on a serving dish.

Place all the other ingredients in a basin and blend by beating together with a pair of chopsticks or a fork for 15 seconds. Pour the 'sauce' evenly over the duck and serve.

This is a Chinese hors d'oeuvre. Or it can be served as a 'wine-accompanying dish' for diners to nibble while they sip their wine.

Sweet and Sour Tripe

(This tripe dish is more sweet than sour; altogether an unusual dish.)

1½ *lbs pig's tripe;* 2 *tablespoons sugar;* 2 *tablespoons lard;* 2 *tablespoons soya sauce;* ½ *cup chicken broth;* ¼ *teaspoon salt;* 2 *tablespoons dry sherry;* 1 *tablespoon vinegar;* 2 *tablespoons chopped coriander; pepper (to taste);* 2 *teaspoons chicken fat.*

Preparation
Boil tripe in a large saucepan of water. Allow to simmer steadily for 2¼ hours. Drain and slice tripe into pieces 1½″ long and ⅙″ wide. Pour into a fresh saucepanful of boiling water to boil for a further 2 minutes and then drain.

Cooking
Heat lard in a large frying pan. Add 1 tablespoon sugar, mix it with the molten lard until the sugar is just beginning to turn

brown. Pour in the tripe immediately to scramble with the sugar/lard. Add salt, soya sauce, balance of sugar, sherry, vinegar, and chicken broth.

Turn the tripe over a few times, and allow it to simmer over low heat for 12 to 15 minutes. Sprinkle with pepper, coriander and chicken fat and serve.

Hot-Fried Salted Duck's Kidney and Intestines

This recipe is reproduced here not so much because of its appeal to the Western palate, but because, as it is very much in the tradition of both Chinese and Peking cooking to use up all the items of the fowl or animal concerned, it will help to show how these often discarded bits and pieces are made into delicacies.

4–5 oz duck's kidney; ½ lb duck's intestines; 1 tablespoon salt; 2 tablespoons vinegar; 3 tablespoons lard; 2 teaspoons sesame oil.

FOR SAUCE
2 tablespoons finely chopped onion; 2 cloves thinly sliced garlic; 2 tablespoons chopped coriander; 1½ tablespoons soya sauce; ½ teaspoon salt; 2 tablespoons dry sherry; 2 tablespoons chicken broth; 1 tablespoon vinegar; 1 teaspoon gourmet powder.

Preparation
Mix the sauce ingredients together in a bowl. Remove the membrane from the kidneys. Use a sharp knife and cut out the gristle. Rinse under running water and drain. Cut each kidney into half.

Scrape off any fat outside the intestines. Cut them in halves with a pair of scissors. Rinse under running water and drain.

Add salt and vinegar to the kidneys and intestines and rub in with the fingers. Leave them to season for 1 hour.

Drop the kidney and intestines into a large pan of boiling water to boil for 15 seconds. Remove and drain them separately. Cut the kidneys with a sharp knife into double matchstick-sized strips. Cut intestines with a pair of scissors into $1\frac{1}{2}''$-segments.

Cooking

Heat lard in a large frying-pan. When it has melted tilt the pan so that it covers the pan evenly.

Add the kidney and intestines, spread them out on the pan, stir and scramble-fry for 15 seconds over high heat. Add the sauce mixture from the bowl into the pan and continue to scramble-fry all ingredients together for 30 seconds. Sprinkle with sesame oil and serve immediately.

TUNG HO CHÜ ('HOME OF HARMONIOUS LIVING')

同和居

The word Chü means 'home' in Chinese. There were originally eight well-known restaurants in Peking called 'Homes'. There are now only two left: Sha Kuo Chu (Home of Earthen-Pot Casseroles), and the Tung Ho Chü (Home of Harmonious Living). The latter is another Shangtung-style restaurant. It was founded in 1901 and is now situated in Fourth South Boulevard West (Hsi Se Nan Ta Chieh).

Royal Concubine Chicken (or Chinese Coq au Vin)

1 *chicken* (3–3½ *lbs*); 2 *tablespoons soya sauce*; 1 *tablespoon sherry*; 2 *large onions*; *oil for deep-frying*.

FOR COOKING AND LATER ADDITION

2½ *pints chicken broth*; 4 *tablespoons sherry*; 3 *tablespoons soya sauce*; 1 *teaspoon salt*; 1 *clove garlic* (*crushed*); 1 *cup* (*large breakfast*) *red grape wine*.

Preparation

Clean the chicken and dry thoroughly. Blend soya sauce and sherry and rub the chicken inside and out with the mixture. Leave the chicken to stand and dry for 15 minutes. Rub again with the same mixture. Leave to dry in an airy spot.

Cut each of the onions into half.

Cooking

Heat oil in the deep-fryer. When very hot immerse the chicken and onion to deep-fry for 5 minutes (2½ minutes on either side). Remove and drain thoroughly.

Place the chicken in a large casserole. Add chicken broth, sherry, soya sauce, salt, garlic and fried onion. Bring to the boil, cover and simmer gently for 1 hour, turning the chicken over ever half hour. Add wine, and continue to simmer for half an hour, then serve in a large serving bowl or in the casserole itself.

Shredded Chicken with Shredded Bamboo Shoots

(This is a 'semi-soup' dish suitable for eating with rice)

½ *lb chicken breasts*; ¼ *lb dried bamboo shoots*; 1 *egg white*; 3 *teaspoons cornflour (blended with 2 tablespoons water)*; 6 *tablespoons lard*; 2 *slices root ginger.*

FOR COOKING AND LATER ADDITION

½ *pint chicken broth*; 2 *tablespoons dry sherry*; ¾ *teaspoon salt*; ¾ *teaspoon gourmet powder*; 2 *teaspoons chicken fat*; ¾ *tablespoon cornflour (blended in 2 tablespoons water).*

Preparation

Soak dried bamboo shoots in water for 1 hour and then shred.

Cut chicken first into slices and then into shreds (as fine as possible). Beat egg white with rotary beater for 10 seconds. Mix well with shredded chicken. Add blended cornflour. Blend well with fingers.

Cooking

Heat lard in a frying pan. When it has all melted, add ginger and fry for 10 seconds over high heat and remove. Drain thoroughly and pour away lard.

Return the pan to the heat. Pour in the chicken broth and add shredded bamboo shoots, salt, sherry and gourmet powder. When the contents boil, stir it around a few times. Add the cornflour mixture. Stir until the liquid thickens. Add the shredded chicken. Turn it over a few times (about 30 seconds). Sprinkle with chicken fat and serve in a tureen or bowl.

The purpose of this recipe is to produce a dish which is simple and refreshing, which is why the main material (chicken) is cooked for so short a time. This dish also goes well with rice.

Simmer-Dried Fried Fish

'Simmer-drying' is one of the most popular processes of Peking cooking. It consists of cooking the main material which has been dipped in batter, for a short period in oil or fat, and then adding broth and other seasoning and flavouring ingredients and sauces. These liquid ingredients are then rapidly reduced. Once they have evaporated and their flavour has impregnated the main materials, the dish is ready.

2 fillets of sole; 1 egg; 2 tablespoons flour; 4 tablespoons lard; 2 slices root ginger.

FOR COOKING AND LATER ADDITION
$\frac{1}{2}$ large cup (breakfast) chicken broth; 2 tablespoons dry sherry; $\frac{1}{2}$ teaspoon salt; 1 tablespoon soya sauce; $\frac{1}{2}$ teaspoon gourmet powder; 2 teaspoons chicken fat; 1 tablespoon chopped parsley.

Preparation
Cut each piece of fish into three pieces, approximately equal in size. Dust with flour, and wet thoroughly with beaten egg.

Cooking
Heat lard in a large frying pan. Add ginger to fry over high heat for $\frac{1}{4}$ minute and then remove. Add the fish, spreading the pieces out over the pan, and fry for $\frac{1}{2}$ minute on either side. Remove to drain, and pour away all the lard in the pan.

Return pan to the heat. Pour in the chicken broth and all the other ingredients. Bring contents to quick boil, lay the pieces of fried fish into the broth (in single layer). After 1 minute reduce heat to low and turn over the pieces of fish. Allow them to simmer until dry.

Sprinkle with chicken fat and parsley and serve in a well-heated dish.

Steamed Carp

1 1½-lb carp (*must be very fresh*); 4 *large dried mushrooms*; 2 *slices root ginger*; 3 *stalks spring onion* (*in 2″ segments*); ¼ *pint chicken broth*; 1 *tablespoon dried shrimps*; 1 *teaspoon salt*; 1 *tablespoon soya sauce*; ½ *teaspoon gourmet powder*; 2 *tablespoons dry sherry*.

Preparation
Scale and clean the carp. Clean thoroughly inside and out. Soak in fresh water for half an hour. Soak mushroom in warm water for half an hour. De-stalk and cut each into four. Drain carp and rub inside and out with salt.

Cooking
Place the fish in a deep-sided oval fireproof dish. Pour in the chicken broth. Arrange the mushrooms, ginger, spring onion segments on top of the fish. Sprinkle evenly with all the other ingredients.

Place the dish in a steamer and steam vigorously for 20 minutes. Remove the two pieces of ginger and serve.

This dish is appreciated for the uncomplicated sweet-freshness of the fish.

The Triple-None-Stuck

This is a well-known Peking sweet, included here mainly to indicate the extraordinary fact that what a Pekingese might call a sweet the average Westerner would merely regard as scrambled egg! What the Pekingese likes about the dish is the fact that it sticks neither to the teeth, nor to the spoon, nor to the chopsticks. Hence its name.

6 eggs; 6 tablespoons sugar; 6 tablespoons cornflour (blended in 6 tablespoons water); 3 tablespoons lard.

Preparation
Beat the eggs, sugar and blended cornflour in a basin with a rotary beater until well mixed.

Cooking
Heat lard in a large smooth frying pan. When it has melted tilt the pan so that the fat will cover the whole of the surface. Pour the excess oil (about two-thirds of it) away into a jug for later use.

Return the pan to the heat (moderate) and pour in the egg-mixture. Stir and scramble-fry for $2\frac{1}{2}$ minutes. Pour in a third of the remaining lard and continue to stir and scramble-fry for half a minute. Repeat twice more with the remaining lard and stir and scramble-fry for half a minute at each addition. Dish out and serve on well-heated plates. (Enough for 4 portions.)

Recommendation
It might be preferable to substitute butter for lard in the West, and to use one or two tablespoons less of sugar. In that case sprinkle the top of the egg when serving with half a tablespoon of rainbow sugar per plate or 1 tablespoon of the chopped fruit glacé so common in Peking.

CH'UNG YÜAN L'OU ('PAVILION OF PRIMARY SPRING')

春元楼

Ch'ung Yüan L'ou is another Shangtung-style restaurant. One of the successors of the original Yuen Ming L'ou ('Pavilion of Luxuriant Brightness'), it is situated in the Tung Hua Men Boulevard. The following recipes are two of its best-known dishes:

Willow Strips of Pork with Five Diced Cubelets in Enriched Tomato Sauce

1 lb pork fillet; 1 egg; 2 tablespoons flour; vegetable oil for deep-frying; 2 tablespoons diced bêche-de-mer (soaked overnight); 2 tablespoons diced bamboo shoots; 2 tablespoons diced ham; 2 tablespoons diced cucumber; 2 tablespoons diced dried mushroom (soaked for half at hour and de-stemmed); 2 spring greens; 2 tablespoons lard.

FOR SAUCE

1 tablespoon sugar; 2 tablespoons tomato puree; 1 tablespoon vinegar; 2 tablespoons dry sherry; $\frac{1}{4}$ teaspoon salt; 1 tablespoon soya sauce; $\frac{3}{4}$ tablespoon cornflour (blended with 2 tablespoons water).

Cut pork into two or three flat slices of about $\frac{1}{4}$–$\frac{1}{3}$" thick. Slash or score both sides of each slice of pork, at intervals of about $\frac{1}{2}$" against the grain. These cuts or slashes should not be deeper than a third of the meat's thickness. Sprinkle and dredge the strips in flour and then wet with beaten egg.

When dicing the bêche-de-mer, bamboo shoots, ham, cucumber, mushrooms, cut them into approximately $\frac{1}{5}$"–$\frac{1}{4}$" cubelets.

Remove outer leaves from the greens and discard. Parboil the hearts for 2 minutes. Drain and cut each green into half.

Mix all the sauce ingredients in a basin and blend well.

Cooking

Heat oil in the deep-fryer. When very hot lower the pieces of pork to deep-fry for 3–$3\frac{1}{2}$ minutes. Remove and drain and cut immediately into approximately 2" $\times$ $\frac{1}{2}$" willow-strip pieces and arrange on a well-heated serving dish.

Meanwhile (or simultaneously) heat lard in a frying pan. Add all the diced cubelets to stir-fry together for $1\frac{1}{2}$ minutes. Pour in the sauce mixture and continue to stir-fry for $\frac{3}{4}$ minute. Then pour the mixture and cubelets over the pork on the serving dish. Arrange the four halves of hearts of green to act as a bank on one side of the dish and serve.

'Triple-White' in Thick Wine Sauce

3 *oz. fillet of white fish (sole, cod, halibut, etc.); 3 oz breast of chicken; 3 tablespoons lard; 2 oz bamboo shoots; 1 egg white; 1½ tablespoons cornflour; 2 teaspoons chicken fat.*

FOR SAUCE

4 *tablespoons 'thick wine sauce' (see page: 82); 1½ teaspoons sugar; ½ teaspoon salt; ½ teaspoon gourmet powder; 6 tablespoons chicken broth; 1 slice root ginger; ¾ tablespoon cornflour (blended in 2 tablespoons water).*

Preparation

Slice fish and chicken breast into thin pieces roughly 1½″ long and ¾″ wide. Wet with beaten egg white and dust with cornflour. Chop root ginger into fine mince.

Cooking

Heat lard in a frying pan. When hot add chicken to stir-fry gently over moderate heat for ½ minute. Remove and drain. Put fish into the pan, spreading the slices over it. Fry steadily for 20 seconds on either side and remove.

Now pour away any remaining fat from the pan. Add bamboo shoots, then chicken broth, salt, ginger, thick wine sauce and sugar. Allow the contents to simmer for ¾ minute, then add gourmet powder and blended cornflour. Stir until the sauce thickens. Whereupon add the sliced chicken and fish. Turn the pieces over gently in the translucent sauce for ¼ minute. Sprinkle with chicken fat and serve.

Triple-Layer Fried Pork and Ham 'Sandwich' with Minced Chicken

1 *breast of chicken; 2 tablespoons pork fat (finely chopped); 1 egg; ¼ teaspoon salt; 4 thin slices of bread (crust removed); 2 slices ham (approximately same size as bread); 2 slices of cooked pork meat (approximately same size as bread); 2 tablespoons chopped parsley; 3 large leaves of lettuce; 2 hearts of spring greens; 2*

tablespoons sweetened bean-paste sauce; vegetable oil for deep-frying.

Preparation
Chop chicken and pork fat into fine mince. Add salt and beaten egg and mix into a paste. Slice hearts of spring greens with a sharp knife into very fine thread-like strips. Mix and toss the latter together into a kind of tangled 'vegetable wool'.

Make two sandwiches by spreading the bread very thinly with the chicken-egg paste. Place sliced ham in between two of the spread pieces, and sliced pork between the other two. Before combining the ham sandwich and the pork one, lay a heavy spread of chicken-egg paste in between them, to act as the middle layer of the Triple-Layer Sandwich.

Cooking
When the sandwich is ready lower it into hot oil and deep-fry for 3 minutes, drain and keep hot. Meanwhile place the shredded, wool-like spring greens to deep-fry in hot oil for 3 or 4 minutes until brown and crispy.

When the crispy greens are ready, cut the sandwich into four, place the pieces on a well-heated dish and sprinkle them with the crispy greens and chopped parsley. Make the lettuce leaves into a bank on one side of the dish and pour some sweetened bean-paste sauce on each leaf so that the sandwiches can be dipped into it with a pair of chopsticks. When all the sandwiches have gone, the lettuce itself, still covered with bean-paste sauce, can be eaten.

This dish has no more than thirty years' history, but is growing in popularity. The chicken-paste, pork and ham give it its central meaty flavour, the fried bread and fried shredded greens its two types of crispiness, the bean-paste sauce its piquancy and the lettuce leaves its freshness.

Five Diced Ingredients Soup

3 tablespoons diced chicken meat (boiled and diced to $\frac{1}{5}''$ cubelets); 3 tablespoons diced dried bamboo shoots (soaked for 1 hour and diced to same size cubelets as chicken); 3 tablespoons diced dried mushrooms (*soaked for* $\frac{1}{2}$ *hour and diced to same size as chicken*); 3 *tablespoons diced* bêche-de-mer (*soaked overnight and diced to same size as chicken*); 3 *tablespoons diced smoked ham* (*diced to same size as chicken*); 1$\frac{1}{2}$ *pints chicken broth*; 2 *tablespoons vinegar*; 2 *tablespoons soya sauce*; 1 *teaspoon gourmet powder*; 1$\frac{1}{2}$ *tablespoons cornflour* (*blended with 2 tablespoons water*); 1 *tablespoon chopped coriander*; *black pepper* (*liberal sprinkling but to taste*); 2 *teaspoons chicken fat*.

Preparation

The five different ingredients can be placed together in a bowl or basin, but they have to be prepared separately and in very good time.

Cooking

Heat chicken broth in a saucepan. When it starts to boil add all the five ingredients, vinegar, soya sauce and gourmet powder. Allow them to simmer gently for 10 minutes. Finally thicken the soup with blended cornflour, sprinkle with pepper, chopped coriander and chicken fat and serve immediately in a large soup bowl or tureen.

Although the preparation of the soup is comparatively simple, it was a famous dish of the original Yung Ming Lou, a celebrated restaurant in Peking. Its appeal lies partly in the contrasting colours of the diced ingredients and partly in the light savoury flavour. The touch of sourness (due to the vinegar) sets the dish in a separate category from any other savoury dishes on the table.

HUNG PIN L'OU ('PAVILION OF CONGREGATING HONOURED GUESTS')

鸿宾楼

Hung Pin L'ou first attained fame in Tientsin (the capital of Hopei) in 1899, and moved to Peking, just outside Ho Ping Men

('Gate of Peace'), in 1955. It is primarily engaged in outside catering and is famous for quite a number of dishes.

Quadruple-Coloured Fish Chowder

½ lb white fish fillet; 4 tablespoons mashed potato; 3 tablespoons carrots (diced to ⅕″ cubelets); 3 tablespoons cucumber (diced to ⅕″ cubelets); 3 large Chinese dried mushrooms (soaked and diced to ⅕″ cubelets); 2 egg whites; ½ pint good chicken broth; 1 teaspoon salt; 2 slices root ginger (cut in fine strips); 1 onion (sliced into fine strips); 2 tablespoons dry sherry; 1 teaspoon gourmet powder; 1 teaspoon sugar; 1 tablespoon lard; 1 tablespoon cornflour (blended with 2 tablespoons water); 2 teaspoons chicken fat.

Preparation
Parboil the diced carrots for 5 minutes and cucumber and mushrooms for 2 minutes and drain. Beat egg whites for ¼ minute with rotary beater. Chop fish with a pair of choppers into a fine paste and place in a bowl.

Add ½ tablespoon lard and 4 tablespoons warm water to the bowl and mix the contents well. Then add mashed potato, half a cup of warm water and salt. Beat all together till it forms a runny mixture.

Cooking
Heat remaining lard in a saucepan. Add onion and ginger to stir-fry for 1 minute and remove with perforated spoon. Pour in the chicken broth. As soon as it boils add the fish-potato mixture. Stir until the contents are well-mixed. Add the sherry, gourmet powder and sugar, and finally all the diced ingredients. Allow them to simmer gently for 10 minutes. Add blended cornflour to thicken. Sprinkle with chicken fat and serve in a large bowl or tureen.

This is not precisely a soup; it is a typical Chinese 'semi-soup' dish, which the diners often spoon on to their rice. It is termed a 'rice-accompanying' dish.

Quick-Fried Diced White Fish

1 lb fillet of fish (sole, halibut, bream, cod, etc.); $\frac{2}{3}$ teaspoon salt; $1\frac{1}{2}$ tablespoons cornflour; 1 egg white.

FOR SAUCE

2 tablespoons lard; $\frac{1}{2}$ teaspoon gourmet powder; $\frac{1}{2}$ teaspoon salt; 3 tablespoons sliced onion; 2 slices root ginger; 1 clove garlic (crushed); 2 tablespoons flour; 4 tablespoons chicken broth; 4 tablespoons milk (or cream); 2 tablespoons white wine; 2 teaspoons chicken fat; 1 tablespoon chopped ham; 1 tablespoon chopped parsley.

Preparation

Dice fish into $\frac{1}{2}$ cubelets. Sprinkle and rub with salt and dredge with cornflour. Beat egg white for $\frac{1}{4}$ minute. Add to diced fish and mix well.

Add fish to a pan of boiling water and simmer for 2 minutes, remove with perforated spoon and drain.

Cooking

Heat lard in a frying pan. When it has melted add onion, ginger and garlic. Stir-fry them together for 1 minute and remove with perforated spoon. Add flour to mix with remaining lard. Stir in the chicken broth and milk gradually, to make a white sauce. Add salt and gourmet powder. Finally add wine and turn diced fish in the white sauce for 1 minute. Sprinkle with chicken fat. Pour onto a well-heated dish, sprinkle with chopped ham and parsley and serve.

One of the attractions of the dish is its striking whiteness.

Soft Braised Sliced Carp

1 lb piece of carp (steak); vegetable oil for deep-frying; $1\frac{1}{2}$ tablespoons lard; 2 tablespoons chopped onion; 1 clove garlic (chopped); 1 teaspoon root ginger (chopped); 1 tablespoon chopped parsley; $\frac{1}{4}$ pint beef broth; 2 tablespoons soya sauce; $1\frac{1}{2}$ teaspoons sugar;

98

1 tablespoon vinegar; 2 tablespoons dry sherry; 3 teaspoons cornflour (blended with 2 tablespoons water); 2 teaspoons sesame oil.

Preparation
Place the piece of carp on a chopping board and cut it through the skin into 10 pieces. Make the cuts on the slant (at about 45 degrees). Heat oil in the deep-fryer and deep-fry the fish for 2 minutes and drain.

Cooking
Heat lard in a frying pan. When it has melted add onion, garlic and ginger to stir-fry in it for 1 minute. Pour in the beef broth and then place the pieces of fried fish evenly over the pan. Sprinkle with soya sauce, sugar, vinegar and sherry and parsley. When the contents boil, allow the fish to simmer gently in the broth for 5 minutes. Then turn it over carefully (so as not to break), and simmer until the liquid in the pan has been reduced to about a quarter. At this point add the blended cornflour, pouring it in gently from all four sides of the pan. Turn the pieces of fish over again carefully. Sprinkle with sesame oil and serve on a well-heated dish. Pour the sauce in the pan over each individual piece of fish.

Shark's Fin in White Chicken Fu-Yung

1 lb sharks' fins; ½ lb breast of chicken; 4 egg whites; ½ cup milk (or ½ cream ½ milk); 1 tablespoon cornflour (blended in 2 tablespoons water); 1¼ pints superior chicken broth; 1 tablespoon lard; 1 medium-sized onion; 2 slices root ginger; 3 tablespoons dry white wine; 1 teaspoon salt; 1 teaspoon gourmet powder; 2 teaspoons chicken fat.

Preparation
Wash sharks' fins in three changes of water. Put in a basin, cover with fresh water and place in steamer for 2 hours. Repeat with

fresh water and steam for one hour. Remove fins from water and drain.

Cut onion into thin slices. Chop chicken breast, rhythmically and patiently, into a very fine mince. Use a pair of sharp choppers and a heavy chopping board. Place minced chicken in a basin, add ¼ pint chicken broth. Pour the resultant mixture through a fine sieve, filtering away any large pieces of chicken. Beat egg whites with a rotary beater until quite stiff. Add the filtered minced chicken to the egg white along with half the salt and gourmet powder. Mix them well together. Finally break or divide the fins into approximately 15–18 pieces (approximately 3″ long strips) and add them to the egg white and minced chicken mixture. Turn the pieces around to mix well.

Heat a pan of water. When it boils place the fins in a wire-basket and lower them to simmer in the boiling water for 1 minute and drain.

Cooking
Heat lard in a large extra-clean frying pan. When it has melted add onion and ginger to stir-fry for 1 minute. Add the rest of the chicken broth. When it boils, stir a few times and remove the onion and ginger. Add milk, white wine, remainder salt, gourmet powder and minced chicken mixture. Stir and finally add the sharks' fins. Allow them to simmer gently together for 5 minutes. Adjust seasoning. Pour the blended cornflour in from all four sides of the pan. Turn the strips of fins over gently. Sprinkle with chicken fat and serve in a large flat shallow tureen.

This dish is distinguished for its pristine whiteness.

CHAPTER FOUR

From the Peking Food-stalls and Barrows

Stuffed Pancake

Originally sold from food-stalls and barrows in market places or at street corners, stuffed pancakes (Hsien Pien) have had over a hundred years of history in Peking. Now they are supplied by numerous food shops and eating establishments. They are usually eaten with soft-rice (congees) or sweetened soft-rice.

FOR PANCAKE
  3 cups (breakfast) flour; 1¼ cups water.

FOR COOKING
  3 tablespoons vegetable oil; 1 tablespoon sesame oil.

FOR STUFFING
  ½ lb beef (steak); ½ lb cabbage (or celery); 2 tablespoons brown bean paste; 1 teaspoon salt; 2 tablespoons finely chopped onion; 2 tablespoons chopped coriander (or parsley); 2 tablespoons sesame oil.

Preparation
Sift flour and add hot water. Mix into a smooth dough. Cover with damp cloth and allow to rise for half an hour. Form into a long 1"-diameter roll. Cut off ¾"-thick discs and roll out into 4"-diameter pancakes.

  Beef is usually reduced to a coarse mince for this recipe: place it in a refrigerator for 2 hours, then cut first into thin slices, then into strips and finally into grains. Cabbage is cut into more or less similar-sized grains. The beef and cabbage grains are then mixed with the other stuffing ingredients into a well-blended mixture.

Hold the dough in the left hand and apply a tablespoon of stuffing with a small bamboo slice (otherwise use the back of a spoon). Gradually work and fold the edge of the pancake over the stuffing with the right hand, while turning the pancake in the left hand. The stuffed pancake is then placed on a board and lightly pressed with hand or rolling-pin into a flat cake.

Cooking
Brush the surface of a frying pan with a mixture of sesame oil and vegetable oil (1 part sesame oil to 3 parts vegetable oil), and place over moderate heat. Place the stuffed pancake to heat for 2 minutes on one side, and then turn over to heat for 3 minutes on the other. Finally turn over again and heat a further 1 to 2 minutes or until brown on both sides. It is eaten as a snack.

Red Bean Soft-Rice

'Soft-Rice' or rice porridge has a social status in China, which, if eaten at any other time than at breakfast, is more or less equivalent to the soup from Victorian soup kitchens. But soft-rice which is sweetened and has red beans added is, however, considered a dainty snack.

$\frac{1}{2}$ *lb rice; 5 pints water; $\frac{1}{4}$ lb red beans; 2 pints water; 4–6 tablespoons sugar (or to taste).*

Preparation
Wash and place rice in 5 pints of water in a very large saucepan. Wash and place red beans in 2 pints of water in a smaller saucepan.

Cooking
Bring rice to boil under cover and simmer gently for $1\frac{1}{2}$ hours (stirring occasionally). Bring red beans to boil and simmer gently

for $\frac{3}{4}$ hour. Combine the two and simmer gently for $\frac{3}{4}$ hour. Add sugar and serve in individual bowls.

This type of rice is both very refreshing in the summer and very warming in the winter. One person can eat two or three bowls of it. (The above quantity should make about 10 bowls.)

Green Pea Soup

The conventional Peking Green Pea Soup is purveyed by food-stalls and often taken at breakfast with hot salted pickles.

$\frac{1}{2}$ lb fresh green peas; 1 pint chicken broth; 1 teaspoon salt;
$\frac{1}{2}$ teaspoon gourmet powder; 1$\frac{1}{2}$ tablespoons cornflour (blended in
3 tablespoons water); $\frac{1}{2}$ teaspoon chilli oil.

Preparation
Add peas to a pint of boiling water to simmer for 10 minutes. Drain and divide into two lots. Mash each lot at high speed in an electric mixer until smooth and creamy.

Cooking
Heat the chicken broth in a large saucepan. Pour in the mashed peas, add salt and gourmet powder and stir. When the liquid starts to boil add the chilli oil and blended cornflour. Continue to stir and simmer gently for 4–5 minutes.

Fried Pasta Beans (or Miniature Dumplings)

'Pasta Beans' are an indigenous type of pasta, which was originally supplied by two family shops in Peking: Madame Mo and her daughter who invented them during the early years of the Republic, and made them popular from their shop, Kwang Fu Kuan ('Shop of Wide Thriving Fortune'), outside the Gate of Peace; and later by a firm called En Yuan Chu ('Home of Original Benevolence') which was situated outside Chien Men, in a city lane called Hutung of Embroidered Hat. Pasta beans are now served as snacks, often from stalls.

4 cups flour; I cup water; $\frac{1}{4}$ lb minced beef; 2 tablespoons chopped onion; I clove garlic (crushed and chopped); $\frac{1}{2}$ teaspoon salt; $1\frac{1}{2}$ tablespoons soya sauce; $1\frac{1}{2}$ tablespoons brown bean paste; 2 teaspoons sugar; 3 teaspoons vinegar; 3 tablespoons vegetable oil; I bowlful coarsely chopped spinach.

Preparation
Add water gradually to flour in a basin. Blend well and knead into a dough. Form dough into strips $\frac{1}{3}$–$\frac{1}{2}$" in diameter. Cut the strips into $\frac{1}{2}$" long segments. Roll each segment in the palm into an elongated egg-shaped nut (or bean).

Heat a large cauldron of water and add all the 'beans' to boil for 5 minutes, stirring all the time. Remove with a perforated spoon and plunge into cold water for $\frac{1}{4}$ minute and drain.

Cooking
Heat oil in a frying pan. Add chopped onion and garlic to stir-fry for I minute over high heat. Add beef and all the other ingredients except for the spinach. Continue to stir-fry for $1\frac{1}{2}$ minutes. Spread the beef out over the pan and pour in all the 'beans'. Mix and stir-fry them together over moderate heat for 3 minutes. Add the spinach and continue to stir-fry for 2 minutes and serve (as a snack). A few tablespoons of diced cucumber are sometimes also added at the same time as the spinach.

Yiu T'iao (or Chinese Doughsticks)

This is served throughout China at breakfast-time and is eaten dipped into soft-rice. Although simple, it is a great favourite with all classes.

I cup (breakfast) sifted flour; 2 teaspoons baking powder; $\frac{1}{4}$ teaspoon salt; $\frac{1}{10}$ teaspoon alum; $\frac{1}{2}$ cup (breakfast) water; oil for deep-frying.

Preparation

Mix all the ingredients in a basin into a smooth dough. Form dough into sticks $\frac{1}{4}$–$\frac{1}{2}''$ in diameter and $6''$ in length.

Cooking

Heat oil in deep-fryer until very hot. Drop the dough-sticks into the oil, two or three at a time, to fry until crisp. Remove and drain.

These doughsticks, which are very light, are delicious in the West dipped in warm or hot milk.

Sweet Mashed Mountain Potatoes

This was originally a southern peasants' dish which was introduced to Peking during the reign of Emperor Chien Lung. It is now a popular snack.

2 lbs mountain potato (or sweet potato); 2–3 tablespoons sugar; 3–4 tablespoons lard (or butter).

Preparation

Peel and cut potatoes into medium-sized pieces (some sweet potatoes are very large). Place in a saucepan of water to heat and boil for 30 minutes. Drain and mash in a basin, adding sugar. Mix and whip until light.

Heat lard (or butter) in another pan. Add the mashed potato. Heat and stir for 3–4 minutes. Serve hot but eat slowly. A more elaborate version of this recipe can be made by adding a small proportion of mashed chestnut (boiled and mashed) to the mashed potato.

Peking Meat and Shredded Carrot Pancake

This particular dish has been popular in Peking for over a century. One of the stalls where it is most celebrated is located in Tung Hua Men High Street, operated by one Liu Kwang Yu. The type of stove used for preparing it was designed to suit the stall. To prepare it in the West the methods have naturally to be somewhat revised and adapted.

1½ *lb flour;* ½ *teaspoon salt;* 10 *oz shredded carrot;* 8 *oz pork;* 1½ *tablespoons sugar;* 2½ *tablespoons soya sauce;* 4 *tablespoons sesame oil;* 2 *medium-sized onions;* 2 *slices root ginger;* 1 *stalk spring onion;* 1 *tablespoon vegetable oil.*

Preparation

THE FILLING

Chop pork into coarse-grained mince. Slice onion into thin slices, spring onion into 1″ segments. Shred carrots into coarse shreds.

Boil carrot in water for 5–6 minutes and drain. Boil pork in water for 2 minutes and drain.

Heat 1 tablespoon vegetable oil and 1 tablespoon sesame oil in a frying pan. Add ginger and onion and stir-fry for 1½ minutes and remove the onion and ginger. Add pork, soya sauce and sugar. Stir-fry over medium heat for 3 minutes, and continue to stir-fry at a reduced heat for a further 5–6 minutes or until the pork is largely dry.

THE PANCAKE

Add ½ pint water to the flour gradually, mix and knead into a consistent dough. Cover with damp cloth and let it stand for one hour. Roll the dough into a sheet 1½ ft in diameter. Brush the top of the sheet all over with sesame oil. Roll it up and flatten with a rolling pin. Brush again with sesame oil. Fold, knead and form into a ball. Finally form the dough into a strip 1½″ in diameter and cut it into 1″ segments. Form each segment into a ball and press the ball with the rolling pin into pancakes of approximately 3″ diameter.

DOUBLE PANCAKE

To fill the pancake, spread on 1 heaped tablespoon of shredded carrot as base. Then heap 1 tablespoon fried pork on top, and cover with another tablespoon of shredded carrot. Cover the filling with another pancake. Secure the edges by pressing them together.

Cooking

Place a griddle or large heavy frying pan on top of medium heat (spread heat with asbestos sheet if available). Place each double pancake on the griddle to heat for 3–4 minutes on either side, until slightly brown. When done, transfer into the oven to bake at 375 degrees (Regulo 4) for 2–3 minutes, when they should be ready to serve. They are normally eaten in Peking as a hot snack (rather like hamburgers in the West).

Peking Biscuit

This recipe was devised comparatively recently, in 1946. Peking Biscuits are sold from a stall at the southern end of Wong Fu Chin High Street (at one time known to Europeans as Morrison Street) by one, Wong Yung Nien. In recent years they have achieved considerable popularity.

> 1½ lbs flour; 1 pint boiling water; 8 eggs; 6 tablespoons sugar; 3 tablespoons butter; 1 teaspoon fruit essence (almond, banana, etc); vegetable oil for semi-deep-frying.

Preparation

Sift flour into a large basin. Add boiling water and mix well with a wooden spoon. When cool, beat eggs and add in 3 stages. Beat and mix well with flour after each addition. Finally add sugar, fruit essence and butter and continue to mix until well-blended. Form the dough (batter) into biscuit-shaped pieces, weighing roughly 1 oz each.

Cooking

Heat ¼ pint oil in a large flat frying pan. When very hot place 4 pieces of biscuit at a time to fry for 3–4 minutes on either side or until lightly brown. Sprinkle with sugar and serve. (The biscuit is meant to be crunchy outside, but still slightly soft inside.)

CHAPTER FIVE

Dishes and Restaurants from the 'Outer Provinces'

All the other provinces of China, except for Hopei and Shantung, are considered by Peking as the 'Outer Provinces'. These include Jehol, Shansi and Shensi to the north and north-west; Kwantung and Fukien, the fruit-laden provinces to the extreme south; Szechuan, the walled-in area of the Upper Yangtze Basin to the extreme west; Hupeh and Hunnan, the 'rice bowls' of China, in the central region; and Kiangsu and Chekiang on the Lower Yangtze to the extreme east. The cooking of the latter region is again divided into two principal schools: the Huai-Yan (Huai River and City of Yangchow) style which emanated from the areas north of the Yangtze, and the Soo-Che style, which is based on the cooking of Nanking, Soochow, Shanghai and Hangchow, the lush silk-weaving cities 'South of the River' which have featured so prominently in the Chinese literary imagination in centuries gone by.

Being capital of China, Peking has been in continuous communication with all these areas for nearly a millennium. Far distinct from trade, there has been a two-way traffic in people: scholars coming up to Peking to attend the Imperial Examinations, and bureaucrats or mandarins travelling from the Capital to govern and administer the outlying areas. This traffic has caused an interchange in culinary delights and traditions, and given the Pekingese some impression of the cooking and dishes of the various regions of China. A number of provincial restaurants have established themselves in Peking, and I have selected some of the dishes for which a number of them are best known.

TU I-CHU

都一处

Tu I-Chu is a Shansi-style restaurant. It was first established in 1738, and has carried on business ever since.

Hung-Cooked Pork

4 lbs fillet of pork; ½ lb bean-curd skin; 5 tablespoons soya sauce; 1 tablespoon sugar; 6 slices root ginger; 5 tablespoons dry sherry; 1 teaspoon gourmet powder; 4 tablespoons flour; small pinch of red colouring; 1½ tablespoons sesame oil; vegetable oil for deep-frying.

Preparation
Cut pork along the grain into pieces measuring 1″ × 3–4″ × ½″. Hang up to dry in a breezy place for 36 hours in the summer and 48 hours in the winter. When ready cut with scissors into 1″ long pieces.

Soak bean-curd skin in warm water for half an hour until soft and cut into similar length pieces.

Mix flour with red colouring and 1 cup water.

Cooking
Bring a large cauldron or saucepan of water (at least 4 pints) to boil. Add the pork to simmer for half an hour. Pour away the water, and rinse the pork under fresh water for one minute. Drain and put aside.

Heat oil in deep-fryer. Lower the bean-curd skin (previously softend by soaking) to fry for 3 minutes, or until brown. Drain.

Heat sesame oil in a large cooking pot. Add ginger to stir-fry for one minute. Add pork and bean-curd skin, soya sauce, sugar, sherry and gourmet powder and continue to stir-fry over high heat for 5 minutes. Stir the flour blended with red colouring and water for a final blending and pour it into the pot. Continue to stir until all the contents are well-mixed and boiling. Pour in sufficient water to cover the meat. Leave to simmer gently for one hour. Serve in a tureen or large bowl.

This dish is over 200 years old. Because the meat has been hung and dried, it has more bite to it than if it had been cooked fresh. It is a rich succulent earthy dish, like the people of Shansi themselves.

Cold Dressed Pork

4 lbs lean pork

FOR DRESSING
$\frac{1}{4}$ *pint dry sherry;* $1\frac{1}{2}$ *teaspoons salt;* $1\frac{1}{2}$ *tablespoons sugar;* $\frac{1}{2}$ *teaspoon cinnamon powder; 2 tablespoons sesame oil; 2 tablespoons finely chopped onion; 2 cloves garlic (chopped); 2 slices root ginger (chopped); 2 tablespoons brown bean-paste; 1 tablespoon soya sauce; 1 tablespoon tomato puree.*
2 tablespoons chopped coriander.

Preparation
Cut pork along the grain into 4 slices. Immerse in water for half an hour. Mix sherry, salt, sugar and cinnamon powder in a basin. Stir and blend well.

Cooking
Bring a large panful of water to boil. Add pork and allow it to simmer for 40 minutes. Drain and allow to cool.

Heat sesame oil in a saucepan. Add onion, garlic and ginger to stir-fry for 1 minute over moderate heat. Add bean paste, soya sauce and tomato puree and continue to stir-fry for another minute. Add the contents from the basin (sherry, etc). Stir and allow the contents to simmer gently for half an hour, or when volume has been reduced to half. Strain the mixture slowly through muslin into a bowl or jug for use as dressing (strain for 20 minutes).

Serving
When the pork has cooled cut it against the grain into very

thin slices. Arrange, slightly overlapping, on serving dish. Pour dressing over the meat, sprinkle with coriander and serve.

This is another dish which has been served in the Tu I-Chu restaurant for over 200 years.

MA K'AI DINING ROOMS

馬凱食堂

The Ma K'ai Dining Rooms are situated in the Ti An Men (or Gate of Earthly Peace) High Street. It specialises in the Hunnan style of cooking, and is famous for its smoked and marinated meats. Hunnan is a mid-Yangtze province, the home of Chairman Mao. Many of its dishes are extremely hot.

Marinated and Smoked Fish, Pork, Chicken and Tongue

At the Ma K'ai Dining Rooms all the cooking is on a massive scale. Over 100 lbs of food are smoked at a time. They are hung over smouldering sawdust in an outside kiln-shaped brick and earth structure for 24 hours. The meat, etc., is first marinated under weight for no less than seven days.

To make the preparation and cooking practicable in an average Western kitchen the process and scale have to be greatly reduced, both in quantity of materials used and time consumed.

1 *large chicken; 1 carp (2–3 lb); 3 lbs pork; 1 tongue (2–3 lb).*

FOR MARINADE
1 *tablespoon salt; 2 tablespoons sugar; 3 teaspoons chilli oil;*
$\frac{1}{2}$ *teaspoon soda; 6 tablespoons sherry; 4 tablespoons brandy.*

Preparation
Clean and quarter the chicken. Cut the fish open from head to tail, and clean thoroughly. Slice the pork into two flat slices.

Mix all the marinating materials together and blend well. Rub each piece of food thoroughly with the marinade twice (after interval of 15 minutes). Place them in a deep jar or bucket. Pour the remaining marinade over them. Place a lid over the food and weigh it down with a 20 lb weight. Leave the food to marinate for 24 hours. Turn the materials over, and continue to marinate under weight for another 24 hours.

Cooking and Smoking
In order not to smoke up a modern kitchen by conducting a prolonged smoking in it, it would be advisable to part-roast and part-smoke the food, a process which is often used in China.

After the ingredients have been marinated for 48 hours, place them on a roasting pan and put into a pre-heated oven to roast at 375 degrees (gas mark 5) for 35 minutes.

Line the bottom of a large saucepan with double duty tin-foil and sprinkle 3–4 tablespoons brown sugar on top. Place the food on a wire frame which stands about a couple of inches over the tin-foil and sugar. Heat the pan over moderate heat until the sugar starts to smoke. Close the lid tight and carry on heating for another 4–5 minutes. Turn off the heat and place the saucepan outdoors. Leave it to stand for half an hour. After half an hour open the lid, remove the food and place the different items on separate dishes.

Final Cooking and Serving
When ready to serve, place any particular item of food in a fire-proof dish and steam vigorously for 20–25 minutes. Slice and serve.

Steamed Four Smoked Items

This dish is a sequel to the previous one. It consists of steaming the four smoked items with additional ingredients, such as sweet-pepper, chilli pepper, salted brown beans, chicken broth, lard and gourmet powder.

3 oz smoked chicken
3 oz smoked pork } *as prepared in the previous*
3 oz smoked tongue } *recipe*
3 oz smoked fish (remove bones). }

2 teaspoons salted beans; 1 sweet pepper; 2 chilli peppers; $\frac{1}{2}$ cup chicken broth; $\frac{1}{2}$ tablespoon lard.

Preparation

Arrange the smoked ingredients, the pieces overlapping, at the bottom of a fireproof dish. Soak salted beans in water for 5 minutes and drain. Cut sweet pepper into eight pieces and each chilli pepper into four pieces each, removing and discarding the pips. Arrange the beans, sweet pepper and chilli pepper on top of the smoked ingredients. Add lard and pour chicken broth over the materials in the dish.

Cooking

Place the dish in a steamer and steam vigorously for 15 minutes. Turn the contents out and arrange the smoked ingredients on top of the peppers in a deep-sided dish.

The hot saltiness of the food is typically Hunnanese in flavour.

Diced Chicken Cubelets Quick-Fried with Chilli Pepper

The purpose of this recipe is to produce a difference of textures: the diced chicken cubelets are slightly scorched outside, but extremely soft and tender inside; they are served up in a savoury hot sauce.

2 breasts of chicken; 3 teaspoons cornflour; 6 chilli peppers; 3 stalks spring onion; vegetable oil for deep-frying.

FOR SAUCE

2 tablespoons soya sauce; 1 tablespoon vinegar; 2 tablespoons chicken broth; $\frac{1}{2}$ tablespoon tomato puree; 2 teaspoons cornflour (blended with 2 tablespoons water); $1\frac{1}{2}$ tablespoons lard; $1\frac{1}{2}$ teaspoons sesame oil.

Preparation

Cut chicken into $\frac{1}{3}''$ cubes with sharp knife. Cut each chilli pepper into 4, remove and discard pips. Cut spring onion into 2'' segments. Sprinkle and rub diced chicken with cornflour.

Cooking

Heat oil in deep-fryer until very hot. Add chicken to fry for 10 seconds, remove and drain. Allow the oil to heat for half a minute. Return the chicken to the oil and fry until slightly brown. Remove again and drain.

Heat lard in a frying pan. When hot add pepper and spring onion. Stir-fry for 1 minute, add soya sauce, vinegar, chicken broth and tomato puree. Continue to stir-fry for $\frac{1}{4}$ minute over high heat. Pour in the blended cornflour water mixture. Stir, and as soon as sauce thickens add the diced chicken. Stir-fry for 10 seconds, add sesame oil and serve.

O MEI RESTAURANT AND O MEI DINING ROOMS

峨 嵋 酒 家

The O Mei Restaurant and Dining Rooms are situated in the East Market. They specialise in Szechuan food, which is distinguished by strongly-flavoured dishes, whether hot, salty, sour or nutty (sesame or peanut-buttery) flavoured.

Tangerine Peel Chicken

1 chicken ($1\frac{1}{2}$–2 lb roaster); $1\frac{1}{2}$ teaspoon salt; 2 tablespoons dried tangerine peel; 3 chilli peppers; 1 medium sized onion; 2 slices root ginger; vegetable oil for deep-frying; $\frac{2}{3}$ tablespoon vinegar; 2 tablespoons soya sauce; 3 tablespoons dry sherry; 2 teaspoons sugar; $\frac{1}{4}$ teaspoon black pepper; 3 tablespoons chicken broth; 1 teaspoon gourmet powder; 2 tablespoons lard.

Preparation

Clean and chop chicken (through bone) into bite-sized pieces. Sprinkle and rub with salt. Leave to season for half an hour.

Slice onion thin. Cut each pepper into four, removing and discarding pips.

Cooking

Heat oil in deep-fryer. When very hot deep-fry chicken in it for 4–5 minutes (divide into lots if necessary) until brown. Drain.

Heat lard in a large frying pan or saucepan. Add onion, pepper, tangerine peel, ginger, to stir-fry over high heat for 3 minutes. Add all the flavouring ingredients (except vinegar).

When contents reboil, add the chicken. Turn the latter over 2–3 times in the sauce, and leave to cook for 6 minutes under cover. Sprinkle with vinegar and serve.

The vinegar accentuates the spiciness. It is an excellent 'wine accompanying' dish.

Szechuan Fried Pork

This is a straightforward dish which can be prepared in a reasonably short time. Although simple it is strong-flavoured and highly spiced.

> 1 *lb pork (leg)*; 1½ *tablespoons soya sauce*; 1½ *tablespoons brown bean paste*; 2 *teaspoons salted soya beans*; ¼ *teaspoon salt*; 2 *slices root ginger*; 1 *teaspoon sugar*; 1 *tablespoon sherry*; 4 *red chilli peppers*; 3 *stalks spring onion (in 1" segments)*; 3 *tablespoons vegetable oil.*

Preparation

Cut pork into thin flat slices, and slice again into pieces 1½" long and ¾" wide. Cut each pepper into four, remove and discard pips. Soak salted beans for 10 minutes, drain and slightly mash.

Cooking

Heat oil in a frying-pan. When very hot add pork and stir-fry over high heat for 2 minutes. Add salt, ginger and peppers and continue to stir-fry for 1½ minutes. Add remaining ingredients: bean paste, salted beans, soya sauce, sugar, sherry. Stir-fry together for a further 1½ minutes.

Finally add the spring onion segments and stir-fry for ½ minute and serve.

Fried-Steamed-Smoked-Marinated Duck

The process of preparing this duck is just the reverse of its title: it is marinated first and deep-fried last. It is time-consuming to prepare, but it has distinctive qualities, which make it an appealing dish as a starter or for accompanying wine. Ideally, the duck should be smoked with sawdust from camphor wood mixed with dried tea-leaves. In Szechuan it is called Camphor-Tea Duck.

> I 2½–3*lb duck; I tablespoon salt; I teaspoon freshly ground pepper; ¼ teaspoon soda; 4 stalks spring onion (in 1″segments); ¼ lb bean sprouts (or 1 cup); vegetable oil for deep-frying.*

Preparation

Mix pepper, soda and salt. Clean duck and rub it inside and out with the mixture. Place in a basin to season for two days. Hang it up to dry for 1 day.

Place the duck on a wire-frame inside a large pan with lid – as in 'Marinated Smoked Fish' (see page 112) to smoke for half an hour (actual heating is for only 7–8 minutes). The material used for smoking in this case should be two tablespoons sawdust mixed with two tablespoons dried tea-leaves.

Cooking

When smoked the duck should be stuffed with the bean sprouts mixed with spring onion, and then placed in a steamer to steam for 1 hour.

After steaming remove the stuffing (which can be used for other purposes), and allow the duck to cool. When cold place it whole in a wire-basket and deep-fry for 10–12 minutes, or until brown.

Serving

The duck can be served hot or cold. It should be chopped through the bone into large bite-sized pieces, and reassembled on the serving dish in the shape of the duck.

The slight smoky flavour with a tinge of spiciness (from the peppers) give the duck a typically Szechuanese flavour.

Fried Fish in Bean-Paste Sauce

2 lbs fish (carp, bream, halibut, turbot, haddock); 3 tablespoons chopped onion; 3 slices root ginger (chopped); 2 cloves garlic (chopped); 3 tablespoons brown bean paste; 1 tablespoon soya sauce; 1 tablespoon vinegar; 2 teaspoons sugar; 2 tablespoons lard; 6 tablespoons chicken broth; 2 tablespoons sherry; ½ teaspoon gourmet powder; 3 teaspoons cornflour (blended with 3 table-spoons water); vegetable oil for deep-frying.

Preparation
Cut fish into thick steaks 2″ × 1½″ × ½″, or chop across the bone and body into ½″ thick pieces.

Cooking
Deep-fry the fish steaks in hot oil for 3 minutes and drain.

Heat lard in a frying pan. Add onion, ginger, garlic, and stir-fry together for 1 minute. Add bean paste, soya sauce, sugar, vinegar. Mix well and pour in the chicken broth and sherry. Stir until the contents reboil. Place the pieces of fish in the sauce. Turn them over, and leave them to simmer over moderate heat until the liquid has been reduced to approximately half. Lift the fish steaks out and arrange on a serving dish. Add gourmet powder and blended cornflour to the pan and stir until sauce thickens. Pour the sauce over the individual pieces of fish.

Szechuan Tossed Noodles (Tan Tan Mien)

½ lb noodles (or spaghetti); ½ lb (or 2 cups) fresh bean sprouts.

FOR SAUCE
2 tablespoons soya sauce; 2 teaspoons vinegar; ½ teaspoon chilli oil; 1 tablespoon sesame jam (or peanut butter) mixed with 1 tablespoon sesame oil; ½ tablespoon lard; 4 tablespoons chicken broth (hot); 1 teaspoon gourmet powder; 1 tablespoon chopped Szechuan pickled cabbage.

Preparation

Mix all the ingredients for the sauce in a large serving bowl or tureen until well-blended.

Cooking

Parboil noodles for 7–8 minutes (spaghetti for 14–15 minutes), and drain. Parboil bean sprouts for 3 minutes and drain.

Serving

Add the hot noodles and bean sprouts to the serving bowl containing the sauce. Toss and mix well.

Noodles Tossed with Shredded Chicken (cold)

$\frac{1}{2}$ *lb noodles (thin noodles or vermicelli); 3 teaspoons sesame oil; $\frac{1}{4}$ lb shredded chicken meat (cooked); $\frac{1}{2}$ teaspoon salt; $\frac{1}{4}$ lb (or 1 cup) bean sprouts; $\frac{1}{2}$ cup shredded cucumber.*

FOR SAUCE

$2\frac{1}{2}$ *tablespoons soya sauce; 1 tablespoon vinegar; 1 tablespoon sesame jam (or $1\frac{1}{2}$ tablespoons peanut butter); 2 teaspoons sugar; 1 teaspoon chilli oil; 1 tablespoon dry sherry; 2 tablespoons salad oil; 1 teaspoon gourmet powder; pepper (to taste); 1 clove garlic (finely chopped); 1 tablespoon spring onion (white); 1 tablespoon spring onion* (green part).

Preparation

Parboil the noodles or vermicelli for 5–6 minutes. Drain and and sprinkle and toss with sesame oil.

Parboil bean sprouts for 3 minutes and drain. Sprinkle chicken with salt. Mix all the ingredients for the sauce in a bowl.

Serving

Place the bean sprouts and cucumber at the bottom of a large bowl as the bed. Spread the noodles on top and the shredded chicken on top of them. Pour the sauce over the noodles and chicken. Toss and mix all together just before eating.

This is a very popular dish in Peking in the summer.

K'UNG TUNG NAN RESTAURANT

康東南菜館

K'ung Tung Nan Restaurant is situated in the Pa Mien Cho, Chung Su Hutung. Although it was not established until 1951, it has become very well-known for its southern foods, such as dishes from Fukien, Kiangsi, Yunnan, etc.

Steeped Kidney in Sesame Butter Sauce

3 pig's kidneys; 4 selected lettuce leaves; 2 teaspoons salt; 4 table-spoons sherry.

FOR SAUCE

2 tablespoons sesame butter (or 3 tablespoons peanut butter); 1 tablespoon salad oil; ½ teaspoon salt; 1 tablespoon soya sauce; 2 teaspoons sugar; ½ teaspoon gourmet powder; ½ teaspoon chilli sauce.

Preparation

Cut out the gristle from the kidneys and remove the membrane. Slice them into razor-thin pieces. Sprinkle with salt, pour half a cup of water and 4 tablespoons sherry over them and leave to soak and season for half an hour. Turn the kidney slices every 5 minutes. Meanwhile mix all the ingredients for the sauce in a bowl.

Drain all the liquid from the kidney slices and place them in a bowl. Pour half a kettleful of boiling water over them, stir and leave to soak for 2 minutes. Repeat a second time (and a third time if kidney still seems somewhat raw).

Serving

Drain the kidney pieces thoroughly. Arrange the lettuce leaves as a bed on a flat serving dish. Place the kidney at the centre of the leaves, and pour the sauce over it.

Because the kidney is very lightly cooked it is extremely crunchy. It is this texture together with the nutty flavour of the sauce which makes for the character of the dish, a typical product of Fukien.

Fish Rolls in Chicken Broth

1 *lb fish (carp, bream, sole, halibut, etc.)*.

FOR FILLING

3 *oz lean pork; $\frac{1}{2}$ egg; 1 tablespoon cornflour; $\frac{1}{2}$ teaspoon salt; 2 teaspoons soya sauce; $\frac{1}{2}$ teaspoon finely-chopped ginger.*

FOR SEALING

$\frac{1}{2}$ *egg; 3 teaspoons cornflour.*

FOR SOUP

2 *pints chicken broth; 1 teaspoon salt; 2 tablespoons dry sherry; 1 teaspoon gourmet powder; 3 teaspoons chopped chives.*

Preparation

Clean and slice fish into razor-thin slices $2\frac{1}{2}''$ long and $1\frac{1}{4}''$ wide.

Mince pork and combine with the other ingredients for the filling. Beat egg and mix with cornflour into a smooth paste. Heat chicken broth in a pan, and add, salt, sherry and gourmet powder.

To make the fish rolls, first spread 1 heaped teaspoon of filling at one end of the fish slice. Roll up the fish and stick down the end with cornflour paste. Arrange all the rolls with the pasted section underneath so that it will stick.

Cooking

When the chicken broth starts to boil, lower the fish rolls one by one into the boiling soup and simmer for 5 minutes. Skim for impurities, and pour the soup and rolls into a large serving bowl or tureen. Sprinkle with chopped chives and serve. Fukien is well-known for its soups, and this is a famous one.

Egg-Slice Soup

This is a dish from the province of Kiangsi, where it is known as 'Egg-Mushroom Chicken Broth Soup'. It came to have this name because when the intestine filled with sliced egg is cooked, it has the shape of a series of mushrooms.

1 *ft length of pig's intestine.*

FOR FILLING
3 *eggs;* 1 *tablespoon dry sherry;* $\frac{1}{2}$ *teaspoon salt;* 3 *tablespoons cornflour;* 4 *tablespoons water.*

FOR SOUP
8 *large dried mushrooms;* 2 *tablespoons shredded cooked ham;* 6 *tablespoons bean sprouts;* $1\frac{1}{2}$ *pints chicken broth;* 1 *teaspoon salt;* $\frac{1}{2}$ *teaspoon gourmet powder.*

Preparation
Immerse intestine in brine (1 tablespoon salt in 2 pints water) for 2 hours. Rinse thoroughly and simmer in boiling water for 1 hour.

Place all the filling ingredients in a basin and beat with a rotary beater for $\frac{1}{2}$ minute. Pour the mixture into the intestine which has been tied with a string at one end. When all the mixture has been poured in secure the remaining end with another piece of string. Soak mushrooms in warm water for 20 minutes. Clean and remove stems.

Cooking
Lower the filled intestine into a pan of boiling water to simmer gently for 10 minutes. Turn off the heat and leave it in the water for a further 4–5 minutes.

Lift the 'sausage' out, drain and place on a chopping board. Slice it (the filling has now solidified) into $\frac{1}{4}''$ thick discs.

Heat the chicken broth in a pan. Add salt, gourmet powder and mushrooms to simmer for 5 minutes. Add the shredded ham, bean sprouts and egg-tripe discs, simmer for a further 3 minutes and serve. This soup is unique in having both real and imitation mushrooms as its constitutents.

Stuffed Mushrooms

10 *large Chinese dried mushrooms;* 1½ *tablespoons lard;* 6–8
tablespoons vegetable oil for semi-deep-frying.

FOR STUFFING
4 *oz finely-minced pork;* 1 *tablespoon dried shrimps;* 1 *slice
root ginger;* 2 *teaspoons cornflour;* ½ *teaspoon salt;* 1 *egg;* 2 *teaspoons soya sauce.*

FOR SOUP (to be reduced in cooking)
1 *cup chicken broth (breakfast cup);* ½ *teaspoon salt;* 1 *tablespoon
soya sauce;* 2 *tablespoons dry sherry;* 1½ *teaspoons sugar;* ½ *teas-
spoon gourmet powder.*

Preparation
Soak the dried mushrooms in warm water for 30 minutes. Drain,
clean and remove stems.

Soak dried shrimps for 30 minutes. Chop and mince together
with finely-chopped ginger. Place them together in a bowl or
basin to blend well with pork, cornflour, salt, soya sauce and egg
into a sticky stuffing. Spread the underside of each piece of mushroom thickly with the stuffing.

Cooking
Heat oil in a frying-pan over high heat, quickly reducing it to
low. Place the mushrooms, underside up, to fry in the oil for 1
minute and then baste with oil for another minute. Remove the
mushrooms and drain away the oil. Return the mushrooms to the
pan, spreading them out in a single layer meat-side down. Pour
in the chicken broth and all the seasonings (sprinkling evenly).
Cover the pan, and gently cook over low heat for 15 to 20 minutes
or until nearly all the liquids have dried. Add lard and turn over
the mushrooms.

Serve on a well-heated dish with the tops of the mushrooms
upward.

Steamed Distilled Chicken

This is a well-known Yunnan dish, and it can really only be cooked and served properly if the special pot used for preparing this dish is available. This pot is constructed like a normal deep-sided casserole, but with a funnel in the centre going through the base of the pot up to the top and with a very small aperture in it just under the lid. This pot is placed in a very large saucepan or cauldron which contains a couple of inches of water. When the water boils, steam rises continually up through the wide-bottomed funnel to be released through the aperture into the pot. Thus, although the chicken and other ingredients are originally packed in dry, they end up, after an hour or two's cooking, swimming in broth produced by distilled water.

A similar effect can be improvised simply by placing dry chopped-up chicken ingredients and seasoning in a fire-proof dish. Then steam it on a raised platform (wire-frame) in a large closed pan or cauldron for 2 hours with 2–3 inches of boiling water. The water is kept at a rolling boil over moderate heat and continually replenished as it becomes reduced. Of course when a proper pot is available the process is very much simplified.

6 pieces of chicken joints; 3 oz cooked ham; 1½ teaspoons salt; 2½ teaspoons sugar; ½ teaspoon gourmet powder; 4 tablespoons sherry; 2 slices root ginger; 6 dried mushrooms.

Preparation
Chop each chicken joint into 3 pieces. Dice ham into ¼″ squares. Soak mushrooms in warm water for 20 minutes and de-stem.

Pack the chicken pieces in the 'moat' of the pot, or, if adapting the method in a separate pot. Sprinkle with seasonings. Arrange the ham and mushrooms on top.

Cooking
Fill a large pan or cauldron with 2½–3″ water and bring to a gentle boil. Stand the pot containing the chicken etc., on a platform over the boiling water, which should be kept at continual rolling boil.

Cover the pan or cauldron and simmer for 2½ hours (replenishing boiling water when necessary).

Serve by bringing the fireproof bowl or 'Chicken Distiller Pot' to the table.

Green and White Soup

This is another soup from Fukien, but it is so thick that it is almost a savoury paste or porridge. It is meant to be eaten ladled onto rice.

GREEN PORTION

> 1 *lb spinach; 1 teaspoon salt; 1½ teaspoons sugar; ½ teaspoon gourmet powder; 2 tablespoons dry sherry; 1 cup chicken broth; 1 tablespoon cornflour (blended in 2 tablespoons water); 2 tablespoons lard.*

WHITE PORTION

> 4 *oz minced chicken meat (white); 6 egg whites; 1½ tablespoons cornflour (blended in 3 tablespoons water); ½ teaspoon salt; ½ teaspoon gourmet powder; 1 tablespoon sherry; 1 cup chicken broth; 1 slice root ginger (minced); 1¼ tablespoons lard.*

Preparation

Clean and remove the stems of the spinach. Chop into a fine mince.

Beat egg whites in a basin with a rotary beater for ¼ minute. Add minced chicken and all the other ingredients for the 'White Portion' of soup (except lard) and beat together for another ¼ minute.

Cooking

Heat 2 tablespoons lard in a saucepan. When it has melted add the minced spinach and stir-fry for 3 minutes over high heat. Add all the other ingredients for the 'Green Portion' and continue to stir-fry gently for another 3 minutes over a low heat. Pour the resulting mixture in from one side of a deep serving dish.

Heat 1½ tablespoons lard in another saucepan. When it has melted add the chicken–egg-white mixture and stir-fry gently over moderate heat for 4 minutes. Pour the mixture in from the other side of the serving dish.

The uniqueness of the dish is that one side of the food is bright green and the other side gleaming white.

HSIAO HSIAO DINING INN ('LITTLE-LITTLE DINING INN')

The Hsiao Hsiao Dining Inn is really a Cantonese 'bistro' situated in the East Market. It is well-known for its snacks, but also for its steamed fish.

The Cantonese Salted-Bean Steamed Fish

1 large 2–4 lb carp or pike (bream or mullet); 1 oz dried bamboo shoots; 5 large dried mushrooms; 4 tablespoons diced (lean and fat) pork; 1 large onion; 2 slices root ginger; 3 tablespoons lard.

FOR THICK SALTED-BEAN SAUCE
2 tablespoons salted brown beans; 3 cloves garlic; $\frac{1}{2}$ teaspoon salt; 2 tablespoons soya sauce; 1 tablespoon sherry; 3 tablespoons chicken broth; 3 teaspoons sugar; 1 teaspoon gourmet powder; 3 teaspoons cornflour (blended with 1 tablespoon water).

Preparation
Clean the fish, dip it in a cauldron of boiling water for 10 seconds and drain.

Slice onion into thin slices. Soak mushrooms and bamboo shoots for 20 minutes and de-stem. Chop mushrooms, pork and bamboo shoots into $\frac{1}{4}$" cubelets.

Soak salted beans in water for 6–7 minutes. Drain, pound and mash in a mortar together with chopped garlic. Add all the other ingredients for the sauce, stir and mix into a paste.

Cooking
Heat lard in a frying pan. Add onion and root ginger to fry in it over moderate heat for 2–3 minutes until brown. Add the mushrooms, bamboo shoots and diced pork and finally the paste to

stir and mix together for half a minute. Place the fish lengthwise on an oval fireproof dish. Spoon the sauce and ingredients evenly over the whole length of the fish. Place the fish in a steamer and steam vigorously for 20 minutes. Serve immediately.

T'AN CHIA TS'AI

譚家菜

T'an Chia Ts'ai is another reputable Cantonese restaurant; it is situated in Hsi Tan High Street, and the following are a few of its better-known dishes.

Cantonese White Cut Chicken

1 2–3 *lb spring chicken; 4–5 oz cooked ham.*

FOR DRESSING
6 tablespoons chicken broth; 1 tablespoon chicken fat; 1 tablespoon oyster sauce; 2 tablespoons dry sherry; 1½ teaspoons powdered mustard; ½ teaspoon salt.

Preparation
Clean chicken thoroughly. Immerse in boiling water for 2 minutes and drain. Slice ham into thin pieces 1½″ long and 1″ wide. Mix and heat the dressing ingredients together until the mixture has boiled for 1 minute and leave to cool.

Cooking
Heat a large pan of water until it boils. Immerse the chicken to simmer for 25 minutes. Drain and allow it to cool. Quarter the chicken and slice chicken breast with a sharp knife off the carcass. Cut each piece of chicken breast into 4 pieces; also cut or chop (through bone) legs and wings into four pieces.

Serving
Spread the wings and leg pieces out as the base on a serving dish.

Arrange the sliced breast meat and ham as an overlapping layer on top. Pour the dressing evenly over the ham and chicken.

Alternatively mustard and oyster sauce can be made into a dip and served in small dishes, instead of being mixed in with the dressing. In this case 2–3 tablespoons oyster sauce and $1\frac{1}{2}$ tablespoons prepared mustard will be needed.

Cantonese Steamed Duck with Ham and Mushrooms

1 3–4 lb duck; 4 oz cooked ham; 10 medium-sized dried mushrooms.

FOR SAUCE-DRESSING
4 tablespoons chicken broth; 1 tablespoon soya sauce; $\frac{1}{4}$ teaspoon salt; $\frac{1}{2}$ teaspoon gourmet powder; 1 teaspoon sugar; 1 tablespoon duck's fat; $\frac{1}{2}$ tablespoon cornflour (blended with 2 tablespoons water).

Preparation
Clean duck thoroughly, remove oil sac, dip in boiling water for 2 minutes and drain.

Soak mushroom in warm water for 15 minutes. Rinse and remove stems.

Cut ham into approximately a dozen thin slices 2″ long and $1\frac{3}{4}$″ wide.

Cooking
Place duck in a deep-sided fireproof dish. Place in a steamer and steam for $1\frac{1}{2}$ hours. Remove duck from steamer and pour any duck soup in the dish into a bowl for later use.

Place duck on a chopping board. Remove head and neck with a chopper. Cut head into half and neck into four. Quarter the duck and carefully slice off the breast meat from the carcass with a sharp knife. Slice breast meat into pieces 2″ long and $1\frac{1}{2}$″ wide (retaining skin). Chop each leg and wing through bone in four pieces.

Place the head and neck pieces in the middle of the fireproof serving dish, and arrange the leg and wing pieces around them.

Arrange the breast meat on top, each piece overlapping alternately with a piece of mushroom and a slice of ham.

Place the dish in a steamer and steam vigorously for a further 15–20 minutes. Meanwhile mix 3–4 tablespoons of the duck soup in the bowl with 3–4 tablespoons chicken broth and the other sauce-dressing ingredients in a small saucepan, heat and stir together for a couple of minutes until it thickens.

Serving
Remove the duck etc., from the steamer, pour the dressing over and serve.

Sesame Seed Steamed Buns

10 oz flour; 2 tablespoons sugar; 2 teaspoons baking powder.

FOR FILLING
4 tablespoons sesame seeds; 4 tablespoons sugar; 2 tablespoons chicken fat (or butter).

Preparation
Sift flour into a basin. Add baking powder. Mix well. Melt sugar in 6 tablespoons boiling water. Add 6 tablespoons cold water to cool. Add the sugar solution to the sifted flour and mix into a dough. Leave it to rise for 1 hour. Divide the dough into 10–12 equal portions and pat each portion into a cake 3–3½″ in diameter.

Spread sesame seeds on a dry frying-pan. Heat and stir over moderate heat until they are aromatic and beginning to turn brown. Place on a clean board, roll and crush with a rolling pin. Place the crushed seeds in a basin. Add sugar and mix well with fat into a smooth filling.

Place a tablespoon of filling at the centre of each dough cake. Bring the sides of the cake over and up evenly until they meet at the top, closing the filling in completely.

Arrange these buns on a cheesecloth spread on top of a fire-proof plate, tray or basket, place in a steamer and steam vigorously for 18–20 minutes.

These steamed buns are eaten as a snack in China.

SEN LUNG INN

森 隆 飯 庄

The Sen Lung Inn specialises in a wide range of dishes from Kiangsu (where Shanghai is situated). It was first established in 1924 in the Chin Yu ('Golden Fish') Hutung and has since achieved a considerable reputation.

Aromatic and Crispy Chicken Legs

10–12 chicken legs; 2 tablespoons cornflour; vegetable oil for deep-frying; 3–4 large lettuce leaves; 1 tablespoon chopped parsley.

FOR MARINADE
2 cloves garlic; 1 tablespoon chopped tangerine peel; $\frac{1}{2}$ tablespoon chopped ginger root; $\frac{1}{6}$ teaspoon five-spice powder; 1 teaspoon salt; 3 tablespoons soya sauce; 1 teaspoon sherry; 2 teaspoons sugar; $\frac{1}{4}$ teaspoon pepper (or to taste); 2 tablespoons sesame oil.

Preparation
Clean and dip chicken legs in a pan of boiling water for 1 minute. Drain and dry. Mix all the ingredients for the marinade well in a large basin. Turn the chicken legs in the marinade until each piece is thoroughly covered. Leave to marinate for 4–5 hours.

Cooking
Arrange the chicken legs in a large fireproof dish and place in a steamer to steam vigorously for 1 hour.

Sprinkle and dredge the legs in cornflour. Place 6 legs at a time in a wire-basket and deep-fry for 4 minutes.

Serving
When both lots of chicken legs are ready, arrange them on an oval serving dish, and serve banked with lettuce leaves and sprinkled with parsley.

Crystal Duck

1 duck (3–3¾ lb); ¼ lb chicken meat; ½ lb pork skin (for gelatine); ½ pint chicken broth; 4 tablespoons dry sherry; 2 teaspoons salt; 1 medium-sized onion; 2 slices root ginger.

Preparation

Remove oil sac, simmer duck in boiling water for 15 minutes and drain. Simmer pork skin in boiling water for 10 minutes and drain. Cut latter into four pieces and chop duck through bone into large bite-sized pieces (approximately 2″ × 1½″). Mince chicken meat.

Cooking

Place pork skin and pieces of duck, the skin-side downward, in a large fireproof bowl. Place onion and ginger on top. Sprinkle with salt and sherry and pour in the chicken broth. Place the bowl in a steamer and steam under cover for 1½ hours (or boil in double-boiler).

Remove the bowl from the steamer. Take out and discard the pork skin, onion and ginger. Pour the duck–chicken broth from the bowl into a saucepan. Remove the duck and re-assemble in a deep-sided oval dish or glass bowl, with skin-side downward.

Add minced chicken to the duck–chicken broth in the saucepan. Bring to boil for 2 minutes. Strain through fine sieve or cheesecloth into a bowl. Allow the filtered broth to stand and cool. When somewhat cool skim away any oil or impurities from the top. Pour this skimmed and filtered broth (which should now be very clear) over the duck in the dish or glass bowl. Place the latter to chill in the refrigerator for 2 hours.

Serving

When ready to serve tip the jellied duck out onto a serving dish. The duck and jelly can be decorated and set off with banked-up green vegetable leaves and flowers. Shrimp sauce, mixed chilli sauce and soya sauce, as well as mixed tomato sauce and soya sauce are often used as dips for this dish.

Fried Fish and Ham Sandwich

1 lb fillet of fish (sole, carp, bream, pike, halibut, turbot, etc.,); ¼ lb ham (sliced); ½ lb pork; 2 eggs; 6 tablespoons cornflour; 3 tablespoons water; vegetable oil for deep-frying; 1 tablespoon chopped spring onion.

FOR MARINADE
½ teaspoon chilli sauce; 2 tablespoons soya sauce; ½ teaspoon gourmet powder; ½ teaspoon salt; 2 tablespoons sherry; 2 slices root ginger (chopped); 1 tablespoon chopped onion.

Preparation
Cut fish with sharp knife into 2"-squares (only ⅙" thick). Mix all the marinade ingredients in a bowl, and marinate the sliced fish in it for half an hour.

Cut ham into slices the same size as the fish, and also the pork.
Beat eggs and blend with water and cornflour into a batter.

When the fish has been marinated dip the slices in the batter, and build a multi-layer sandwich by placing a slice of fish on top of a piece of pork, then a slice of ham and finally another slice of fish.

Cooking
Place these 'sandwiches' in a wire-basket and sink them in hot oil to deep-fry for 2½ minutes and drain. Heat 4 tablespoons oil in a large frying pan. Heat over high heat for 1 minute and pour away the oil. Arrange the 'sandwiches' in the frying pan, spreading them over the pan evenly, pork side facing down. Heat over low heat for 4–5 minutes until the pork is brown. Arrange on well-heated dish, sprinkle with onion.

Serve hot. An excellent 'wine-accompanying' dish.

Dry-Cooked Giant Prawns

6 giant prawns (approximately ⅛ lb to ¼ lb each); ½ teaspoon salt; 2 tablespoons chopped onion; 2 slices root ginger (chopped); 2 cloves garlic (chopped); 1 tablespoon salted beans; 2 tablespoons vegetable oil; 1½ tablespoons lard.

FOR SAUCE

> 2 tablespoons dry sherry; 4 tablespoons chicken broth; 3 teaspoons vinegar; $1\frac{1}{2}$ tablespoons soya sauce; 2 teaspoons chopped hot Szechuan pickled cabbage; $\frac{1}{2}$ teaspoon gourmet powder; $1\frac{1}{2}$ tablespoons tomato puree.

Preparation

Rinse prawns several times in fresh water. Remove head and cut lengthwise through the shell, remove the dark line in the back. Rinse once more and drain. Sprinkle meat-side of prawns with salt.

Mix and blend the ingredients for sauce in a bowl.

Cooking

Heat oil in a frying pan. Add onion, ginger, salted beans and garlic to stir-fry for $1\frac{1}{2}$ minutes over high heat.

Add prawns. Stir-fry gently for 2 minutes over high heat. Pour the sauce mixture in evenly over the pan. Turn the prawns in the sauce once. Reduce heat to moderate, and allow the prawns to simmer in the sauce until the latter is almost dried. Add lard. Turn the prawns in the molten lard two or three times and serve.

YÜ HUA DINING ROOMS

正華食堂

Yü Hua Dining Rooms are in the Tung Chao Min Hsien, an area which used to be called the Legation Quarter in the old days. The restaurant is well-known for its Huai-Yang cooking (North Yangtze) and famous for its extensive menu.

Barbecued Stuffed Duck

1 duck (3–4 lbs); 4 tablespoons sugar-water ($1\frac{1}{4}$ teaspoons sugar melted in the water).

FOR STUFFING
  4–5 sheets dried lotus leaves; 2 large onions; 4 slices root ginger; $\frac{1}{4}$ teaspoon black pepper; 2 teaspoons salt.

Preparation
Clean duck thoroughly inside and out. Wipe and dry with a cloth. Remove head, neck and oil sac.

Soak lotus leaves in hot water for 2 minutes (to soften). Cut each piece into a dozen smaller pieces. Chop onion and add to the lotus leaves, along with ginger, pepper and salt. Mix them up evenly. Stuff the cavity of the duck with the mixture.

Pass the skewer through the duck from tail to front (secure the duck onto the skewer by tying it if necessary). Pour 2 kettles of boiling water over the duck. Wipe and place the duck in an airy spot for 5–6 hours.

Cooking
Just before grilling or barbecuing the duck, rub its skin all over with sugar-water.

Fix the skewer into the rôtisserie to roast under moderate heat for approximately $\frac{3}{4}$–1 hour, until the skin is deep brown.

Serving
As with Peking Duck the skin of the duck, which should now be crispy and crackling, should be sliced off and eaten first, and then the meat (the stuffing is there only to provide an aromatic effect).

Normally the skin and meat of the duck are eaten wrapped in thin pancakes along with raw cucumber strips and spring onion segments heavily brushed with sweetened bean-paste or plum sauce. (Sweetened bean-paste can be prepared by heating and mixing 4 tablespoons bean paste with $1\frac{1}{2}$ tablespoons sugar and $1\frac{1}{2}$ tablespoons sesame oil over low heat for 5–6 minutes.) Or they can be eaten in conjunction with Steamed Rolls (See page 69).

Eight Precious Stuffed Chicken

The chicken or capon is here stuffed with eight ingredients.

At the restaurant the bird is first of all de-boned without damaging the skin even slightly. As doing this requires expertise beyond the average, in this recipe we shall stuff the chicken in the normal way without any over-elaborate preparation.

I *capon* (3–4 *lbs*); 6 *oz dried Chinese mushrooms*; 2 *oz* (or $\frac{1}{4}$ *cup*) *dried bamboo shoots*; 2 *medium-sized onions* (*sliced*); 2 *slices root ginger*; 2 *tablespoons soya sauce*.

FOR STUFFING

4 *large dried Chinese mushrooms*; 2 *oz dried bamboo shoots*; 2 *oz cooked ham*; 4 *tablespoons cooked lotus seeds*; 4 *tablespoons pine kernels*; 2 *tablespoons dried scallop muscles*; 3 *tablespoons glutinous rice*; 3 *tablespoons green peas*; I *pair chicken kidney and liver*; 2 *tablespoons dry sherry*; I *teaspoon salt*; $\frac{1}{2}$ *teaspoon gourmet powder*.

FOR GRAVY

I *teaspoon sugar*; $\frac{1}{2}$ *teaspoon gourmet powder*; I *tablespoon soya sauce*; I *teaspoon shrimp sauce*; 3 *teaspoons cornflour* (*blended in* 2 *tablespoons water*); I *tablespoon lard*; 6 *tablespoons chicken broth*.

Preparation

Clean chicken thoroughly inside and out. Dip it in boiling water for $\frac{1}{2}$ minute and drain.

Prepare stuffing by washing and soaking lotus seeds and glutinous rice in water for 10 minutes and drain. Soak mushroom and bamboo shoots in warm water for 20 minutes and dice into $\frac{1}{6}''$ cubelets together with ham, chicken liver and kidney. Soak the last three items in boiling water along with scallops for 3 minutes and drain. Place all the ingredients for the stuffing in a bowl and mix well.

Stuff the chicken with the mixture and secure by sewing with thread.

Cooking

Place the stuffed chicken in a casserole which is only slightly bigger than the chicken. Add onion, ginger, mushrooms, bamboo shoots and soya sauce and then pour in sufficient water to just cover. Bring to gentle boil and simmer for a further 1½ hours.

Serving
Lift the chicken out from the casserole and transfer it on to a large well-heated serving plate. Remove thread. Place onion, mushrooms and bamboo shoots in a small pan, to heat with other ingredients for the gravy for 2 minutes. Then pour the gravy over the bird.

Dried-Cooked Fresh Fish

1 2lb crucian carp (bream, 2 trout or 3 fat herrings); 1 tablespoon vegetable oil; 2 tablespoons diced pork suet; 1 onion (sliced); 2 slices root ginger; 1 teaspoon salt; 2 tablespoon lard; 1 tablespoon chopped parsley.

FOR SAUCE
4 large Chinese dried mushrooms (soaked 20 minutes, shredded); 4 oz dried bamboo shoots (soaked 20 minutes, shredded); ¼ pint chicken broth; 2 tablespoons soya sauce; 2 tablespoons sherry; 1 tablespoon vinegar; 1½ teaspoon sugar.

Preparation
Clean fish thoroughly. Rub with salt inside and out. Mix the ingredients for the sauce in a bowl. Dice the pork suet in ⅛" cubelets.

Cooking
Heat oil in a frying pan. Add suet cubes and stir-fry for 1 minute. Add onion and ginger and stir-fry for a further minute. Push these ingredients aside, place the fish in the middle of the pan and pile them back on top of the fish. Fry the fish for 3 minutes on either side over high heat. Pour away excess fat.

Pour the sauce mixture into the pan. When it boils turn the fish (or fishes) over in it once. Reduce the heat to low, and allow the contents of the pan to simmer gently until nearly dry.

Add lard, turn the fish over in it, sprinkle with parsley and serve.

Crystal Prawn Cakes

It is typical of the tradition of Chinese poetic culinary licence to call these prawn cakes 'crystal', for they are really only slightly translucent.

$\frac{2}{3}$ *lb prawn meat; 2 oz pork fat; 2 oz potato; 2 oz water-chestnut; 2 eggs; 1 tablespoon cornflour (blended in* $1\frac{1}{2}$ *tablespoons water); 1 medium-sized onion; 2 slices root ginger;* $\frac{3}{4}$ *teaspoon salt;* $\frac{1}{2}$ *teaspoon gourmet powder; vegetable oil for deep-frying.*

FOR DRESSING

2 tablespoons chicken broth; 2 tablespoons vinegar; 2 teaspoons sugar; 1 tablespoon soya sauce.

Preparation

Chop and mince prawns, pork fat, potato and water-chestnut into small-grained mince. Place them together in a basin. Add beaten egg and mix to an even consistency.

Chop onion and boil it in 6 tablespoons water, along with ginger, until water is reduced to half. Pour the water through a sieve onto the salt in a bowl so that it dissolves. When the water has cooled add it to the prawn mixture. Finally add cornflour and gourmet powder. Stir and mix until well-blended. Place the mixture in a refrigerator for 1 hour to set.

When the mixture is quite firm form it into 1″ diameter balls, and then press them into 2″ diameter cakes.

Cooking

Heat the oil in a deep-fryer. When hot place the prawn cakes (6 at a time) to deep-fry for 1 minute over high heat, which is immediately reduced to low-moderate heat for 2 minutes, finishing off with $\frac{1}{2}$ minute of frying at high heat. Drain and keep hot in an oven while the other prawn cakes are being fried. When all are ready, arrange on a well-heated dish.

Serving

Sprinkle with the dressing previously mixed in a bowl or jug.

PART THREE

Home-Cooked and
Other Dishes

require outsize or specialised pieces of equipment which are not part of the normal kitchen (such as the brick-oven for Peking Duck, the outsize stockpot and master-sauce pot, 20 gallon deep-boiling cauldron, and so on.)

However, if there is any difference between home cooking and restaurant cooking, it probably lies in emphasis. Home-cooked dishes are more likely to be 'rice-accompanying', since more rice naturally is eaten at home; restaurant dishes tend more to be 'wine-accompanying', since more wine and less rice (if any at all) are served in restaurants. Furthermore, home-cooked food is often meant for more than one meal, since that saves time; while in restaurants, dishes are always produced to be consumed on the one occasion. For this reason probably the bulk of restaurant dishes are quick-stir-fried, a process which produces a dish in an instant, and also gives the chef the maximum opportunity to display his virtuosity. This, of course, does not mean that there are no long-cooked dishes in restaurants – indeed, some restaurants specialise in them – but in the main these dishes are in the minority, and tend more to belong to the sphere of home-cooked food.

Pickled, salted, jellied, smoked and wine-marinated dishes are all meant to keep. They are very common in the home, and are served with the universal breakfast soft-rice (congee); they also form part of 'midnight suppers' when lengthily-heated, elaborate dishes are seldom eaten (in much the same manner as people in the West simply go to the refrigerator for snacks when they return late after a night out). However, since the range of 'cold dishes' in the Chinese repertoire is so excellent, they are used extensively as 'starters' to a Chinese dinner party or banquet. They can also be easily served as hors d'oeuvres and canapés in the West.

Home-cooked dishes, of course, also contain a wide range of more simply-cooked dishes. These use the more readily available flavourings and ingredients, some of which, being seasonal, are at certain times in great abundance. This applies especially to vegetables and seafoods. Meat and poultry are, of course, available all the year round; these are either used simply or in combination with other basic ingredients. In the households where economy not only counts but is of primary importance, the latter form of dishes must predominate. All the same, because of the huge quantity of rice and plain steamed buns consumed, all Chinese dishes, whether pure meat, vegetable or mixed-up combinations, have to be highly savoury in order to set off the blandness of these basic foods. It is this tastiness which makes Chinese food so appealing to Westerners. It is as essential to Peking food as to any Chinese regional cooking, to home-cooked food as to restaurant-cooked dishes.

COLD DISHES
(SUITABLE FOR STARTERS)

冷盤

Crispy Fish

2½ lbs herrings, sardines (or other small fish); 3 medium-sized onions; 3 cloves garlic; 3 slices root ginger; 1 small piece dried tangerine peel; 4 tablespoons sugar; 4 tablespoons soya sauce; 6 tablespoons vinegar; 6 tablespoons dry sherry; 1½ pints chicken broth (or bone broth); 1 drop red colouring.

Preparation
Scale and clean the fish thoroughly and place in a heavy pan or casserole. Cut onion into thin slices and crush garlic, then place both in a cloth bag with ginger and tangerine peel.

Cooking
Pour broth into the fish in the casserole. Add cloth bag containing the different ingredients. Add sugar, soya sauce, vinegar and sherry. Bring contents to gentle boil. Simmer gently for 1 hour. Remove cloth bag. Add red colouring. Continue to simmer gently until all liquid has dried.

The distinctive quality of the dish is that, although the fish are still intact, their bones, after the prolonged simmering (especially with all the vinegar and sugar) have become soft and highly edible. As the result of the ingredients used, the fish themselves are extremely delicious and crispy.

Coral Fish

1½ *lbs fish steak (sole, bream, carp, cod, pike etc.); 1 teaspoon salt; 2 tablespoons dry sherry; vegetable oil for deep-frying.*

FOR SAUCE

1 onion; 2 slices root ginger; 1 red sweet pepper; 2 red chilli peppers; 1 tablespoon tomato puree; 1 tablespoon soya sauce; 1 tablespoon sugar; ½ teaspoon salt; ½ teaspoon gourmet powder; 2 tablespoons dry sherry; ¼ pint chicken broth; small drop red colouring; 2 tablespoons sesame oil.

Preparation

Cut fish into strips 2″ long and ¾″ wide. Sprinkle and rub with salt and sherry.

For the sauce, shred onion, ginger, sweet pepper and chilli pepper (removing pips from the peppers). Mix in a basin, tomato puree, soya sauce, sugar, salt, gourmet powder, sherry, chicken broth and red colouring.

Cooking

Place seasoned fish in a wire basket. Lower into boiling oil to deep-fry for 1½ minutes and drain.

Heat sesame oil in a large frying pan. Add onion, ginger, sweet pepper and chilli peppers to stir-fry over high heat for 2 minutes. Add all other ingredients of the cooking sauce. Stir until they boil. Add the fish into the sauce and spread it out evenly over the pan. Turn the pieces over carefully once or twice, and leave them to simmer over moderate heat until the sauce is nearly dried up.

Serve hot or cold.

Smoked Prawns

10 *giant prawns.*

FOR STOCK

2 medium-sized onions; 1 teaspoon black peppercorns; 3 slices root ginger; 1½ teaspoons salt; 3 teaspoons sugar; 3 tablespoons dry sherry; ½ pint bone broth; ½ teaspoon gourmet powder.

FOR SMOKING
   3 heaped tablespoons sawdust; 2 tablespoons tea-leaves (dried).

FOR SERVING
   2 tablespoons sesame oil.

Preparation
Clean prawns thoroughly. Remove the head and legs of the prawns, pick out the dark line from the backs by slicing open the shell with a sharp knife (without removing the shell).
   Quarter the onions and crush the peppercorns with the side of a chopper.

Cooking
Heat all the ingredients for the stock in a large saucepan and bring to boil. Add the prawns (discarding the other ingredients) and simmer until the stock is nearly dried.

Smoking
Place the prawns in a wire-basket which in turn is placed on a raised platform inside a large pan (see page 112) The sawdust and dried tea-leaves are mixed and placed on top of a sheet of tinfoil at the bottom of the pan. Place the pan over moderate heat until the sawdust and tea-leaves begin to smoke. Continue to heat for a further 5 minutes under a tight-fitting lid. Take the pan outdoors and allow the prawns to smoke inside the pan for 10 more minutes.

Serving
Remove prawns from the wire-basket inside the smoking pan and place on serving dish. Brush each prawn with sesame oil and serve.

Smoked Liver

Use 1½ lbs of liver and the same quantities of ingredients as in the previous recipe.
   Proceed almost exactly as in the previous recipe, except that

143

one piece of dried tangerine peel and one anise star are added to the stock during the simmering; also the liver is sliced only after having being smoked and then brushed with sesame oil. For refinement the liver is dipped in boiling water for 3 minutes and drained before immersion in the stock.

Tossed Chicken Threads with Shredded Cucumber and Sweet Pepper

$\frac{1}{2}$ *lb breast of chicken; 1 egg white; $\frac{1}{2}$ teaspoon salt; 1 tablespoon cornflour; oil for deep-frying; 1 6" long piece of medium-sized cucumber; 1 red sweet pepper; 1 red chilli pepper; 1 tablespoon soya sauce; 1 tablespoon sherry; 1 teaspoon sugar; 2 oz transparent pea-starch noodles.*

FOR DRESSING

$1\frac{1}{2}$ *tablespoons sesame oil; $1\frac{1}{2}$ tablespoons soya sauce; 1 tablespoon sherry; 1 tablespoon vinegar; 2 tablespoons concentrated chicken broth; $\frac{1}{4}$ teaspoon salt; $\frac{1}{4}$ teaspoon gourmet powder.*

Preparation

Shred chicken into fine threads. Beat egg white with a fork together with salt and cornflour for half a minute. Add chicken and mix well together.

Shred peppers, discarding pips, into matchstick-sized strips. Cut cucumber into three 2" long segments, and then slice lengthwise into double matchstick-sized strips.

Simmer pea-starch noodles for 3 minutes in boiling water and drain.

Cooking

Spread the chicken threads and deep-fry or semi-deep-fry for $1\frac{1}{2}$ minutes in boiling oil and drain.

Stir-fry sweet pepper and chilli pepper in 2 tablespoons oil for 1 minute over high heat. Add soya sauce, sherry and sugar and continue to stir-fry for a further minute over moderate heat and drain.

Serving

Place the noodles at the bottom of a round serving dish. Scatter the white chicken threads on top. Place the red peppers on top of the middle of the chicken, and surround them with green cucumber strips. Pour the dressing over them.

Serve cold. When ready to eat, toss and mix the various constitutents together. An exceptionally attractive dish.

Jellied Lamb

2 lbs lamb (leg); 4 oz radish; 2 medium-sized onions; 2 slices root ginger; 2 cloves garlic; 1 tablespoon dried tangerine peel; 1 anise star; 2 pints chicken broth; 3 tablespoons dry sherry; 2 teaspoons sugar; 2 tablespoons soya sauce; 1 teaspoon salt; 1 teaspoon gourmet powder; 4 oz pork skin (for gelatine).

Preparation

Peel and cut radishes and onions into quarters. Crush garlic and soak tangerine peel in water for 20 minutes.

Parboil lamb in boiling water for 5 minutes and drain.

Cooking

Place lamb in a large heavy saucepan with chicken broth and bring to boil. Add onion, ginger, garlic, radish, tangerine peel and anise star, all in a cloth bag (bouquet garni). Add pork skin and all the seasonings: sherry, sugar, salt, soya sauce and gourmet powder. Simmer altogether for 35 minutes over low-moderate heat.

Remove the cloth bag with all its contents. Take the lamb out and place in a deep-sided dish. Skim broth of oil and other impurities. Chop and mince pork skin into tiny grains, and put them back into the saucepan for 15 minutes' simmering. Filter the broth through muslin over the lamb. Let cool and place the dish in the refrigerator for 2–3 hours to jell.

Serving

Take the lamb out and slice into strips measuring $1\frac{1}{2}'' \times \frac{1}{2}''$. Serve with the jelly.

Although served cold it is a favourite Peking winter dish.

POULTRY

鶏鴨

Crystal Duck

Crystal Duck is prepared in very much the same manner as Jellied Lamb. Pork skin is again used as the jellifying agent (although in the West gelatine can be substituted).

1 duck (2–3 lb); ¼ lb minced chicken meat; 4–5 oz piece of pork skin; 1½ pints chicken broth; 1½ teaspoons salt; 1 teaspoon gourmet powder; 3 tablespoons white wine; 2 slices root ginger; 1 medium-sized onion (in thin slices); 2 stalks spring onion (1″ segments).

Preparation
Clean and chop duck through bone into approximately 20 pieces.
Parboil pork skin in boiling water for 5 minutes and cut into four.

Cooking
Place duck pieces in a deep-sided dish, skin-side down. Add pork skin, onion and ginger, sprinkle with salt, and pour in the chicken broth. Close the top of the dish with tin-foil and place in steamer to steam for 1½ hours.

Remove dish from steamer, discard onion, ginger and pork skin. Pour the duck-chicken broth into a separate pan. Skim for excess oil and impurities. Add minced chicken, bring to boil and simmer for 3 minutes. Pour through filter and muslin and skim again for oil and impurities. By this time the resultant broth should be crystal clear.

Sprinkle duck with spring onion segments and pour the clear broth over it. Add white wine and gourmet powder. Return dish to steam under cover (tin-foil) for another 10 minutes.

Allow the dish to cool for 25–30 minutes and then place in a refrigerator for 2–3 hours to jell.

Serving
When ready to serve turn the duck and jelly out onto a serving

dish. Decorate with any suitable fruits and vegetables and serve. Shrimp sauce is often used as a dip for this dish.

Steamed Chicken in Wine

1 *chicken (2–3 lb); 4 stalks spring onion; 3 slices root ginger; 1½ teaspoons salt; ½ pint white wine; ¼ pint dry sherry; 2 teaspoons cornflour (blended in 1 tablespoon water); ½ teaspoon gourmet powder.*

Preparation
Clean chicken thoroughly, Dip in boiling water for 3 minutes and drain. Rub chicken with salt inside and out and place in a deep-sided fireproof dish. Cut spring onions into 2″ segments and each slice of ginger into two. Stuff the chicken with half the onion and ginger, pour the wine over it and spread the remainder of the onion and ginger on top.

Cooking
Place the dish in a steamer and steam for 45 minutes. Turn the chicken over, pour in the sherry and steam for a further 35 minutes.

Serving
Transfer the chicken into a deep-sided serving dish. Pour about ¼ pint of the chicken broth in the fireproof dish into a pan. Add gourmet powder and blended cornflour. Heat and stir for 3 minutes and pour the sauce over the chicken. The latter should be sufficiently tender to be taken to pieces at the table with a pair of chopsticks.

Steamed Duck in Wine

Repeat the preceding recipe substituting duck for chicken.

Fried Chopped Chicken

1 *spring chicken (about 2 lbs); 2 teaspoons salt; 1½ tablespoons dry sherry; ½ teaspoon gourmet powder; 1 egg; 2 tablespoons cornflour; vegetable oil for deep-frying.*

Preparation
Chop chicken through bone into large bite-sized pieces. Sprinkle with sherry and rub with salt and gourmet powder. Leave to season for one hour.

Beat egg in a basin. Dip chicken pieces in the beaten egg. Sprinkle and dredge with cornflour.

Cooking
Heat oil in deep-fryer. When very hot divide the pieces of chicken into three lots and deep-fry each lot for 4 minutes. Pile them on a well-heated serving dish, sprinkle with salt and pepper and serve.

Triple Shreds

3 oz chicken breast; 3 oz smoked chicken; 3 oz roast duck; 1 egg white; 1 tablespoon cornflour; 2 stalks spring onion; ¾ teaspoon salt; ½ teaspoon gourmet powder; 2 tablespoons chicken fat; 4 tablespoons chicken broth; 1½ tablespoons sherry.

Preparation
Slice breast of chicken with sharp knife into double matchstick-sized strips. Beat egg white with rotary beater for 15 seconds. Add cornflour and beat for a further 15 seconds. Add shredded chicken to mix with the cornflour egg-white mixture.

Cut spring onion into 2" segments.

Cut roast duck and smoked chicken into neat double-treble matchstick-sized strips.

Cooking
Heat chicken fat in a frying pan. When hot, add shredded chicken, spreading it evenly over the pan. Stir-fry for 1 minute. Add spring onion segments, followed by shredded duck and smoked chicken. Sprinkle with salt, gourmet powder, chicken broth and sherry. Stir-fry for 3 minutes. Dish out onto a well-heated dish and serve.

This dish is an interesting mixture of flavours and is also useful when there are leftovers of chicken and duck.

148

Chicken Fu-Yung Slices

Despite its name, this dish is only partly made with chicken.

3 tablespoons finely-minced chicken breast; 3 tablespoons finely-minced cooked white fish (sole, cod, etc); 2 tablespoons mashed potato; 4 egg whites; 2 tablespoons chicken broth; 1 teaspoon finely chopped onion; ½ teaspoon finely-chopped root ginger; ½ teaspoon salt; vegetable oil for deep-frying.

FOR SAUCE
6 tablespoons chicken broth; ½ tablespoon cornflour (blended with 1½ tablespoons water); ½ teaspoon gourmet powder; ¼ teaspoon salt; 1 tablespoon white wine.

Preparation
Beat egg whites with a fork for 1 minute. Add minced chicken, fish, mashed potato, chicken broth, onion, ginger and salt. Continue to beat (in one direction) with a fork until the mixture is consistent.

Mix the ingredients for the sauce in a bowl.

Cooking
Heat oil (which must be absolutely clean) in a deep-fryer. Slide spoonfuls of the mixture of minced chicken etc. (a spoonful at a time) into the hot oil from the side of the pan. On meeting the hot oil the mixture spreads out into a thin slice. Turn it over with a spoon and lift it out with a perforated spoon after 12 seconds' frying. Repeat until all the mixture is used up.

Heat and stir the sauce mixture in a separate frying pan. Slide all the 'chicken' fu-yung slices into the sauce. Turn them over in the sauce with a slice. Serve as soon as the contents start to boil.

MEAT DISHES

肉類

Quick-Fried White-Cooked Pork

2 lbs pork (⅔ lean); 1 green sweet pepper; 1 teaspoon salt; 1½ tablespoons flour; vegetable oil for deep-frying.

FOR SAUCE (THICK)

2 tablespoons soya bean paste; 1 teaspoon chilli sauce; 1 tablespoon soya sauce; 1½ tablespoons dry sherry; 2 teaspoons sugar; ½ teaspoon gourmet powder; 2 tablespoons lard.

Preparation

Parboil pork in boiling water for 10 minutes. Drain, cool and slice into double matchstick-sized strips. Cut green pepper into similar-sized strips, removing pips.

Sprinkle pork strips with salt, and dredge in flour. Rub flour and salt evenly into the pork.

Cooking

Heat oil in the deep-fryer. When very hot deep-fry the pork in it for 2½ minutes, remove and drain.

Heat lard in a frying pan. Add sweet pepper and stir-fry for 1 minute. Add all the ingredients for the cooking sauce. Stir over high heat until most of the moisture has evaporated. Pour in the pork, stir and mix with the sauce and pepper for 1½ minutes and serve.

Quick-Fried Diced Pork in Soya Bean Paste

2 lbs pork (⅔ lean); 1 egg; 1½ tablespoons cornflour; 5 tablespoons vegetable oil; 1 teaspoon finely-chopped root ginger; 1 tablespoon finely-chopped onion.

FOR SAUCE (THICK)

2 tablespoons chicken broth; 2 tablespoons soya bean paste; 1 tablespoon soya sauce; 1½ tablespoons dry sherry; 2 teaspoons sugar; ½ teaspoon gourmet powder.

Preparation

Dice pork into cubes of ¼–⅕". Beat egg in a bowl for 10 seconds with a fork. Dip pork in egg, sprinkle and dredge in cornflour.

Mix all the sauce ingredients in a bowl.

Cooking
Heat 3 tablespoons oil in a frying pan over high heat. Add the pork and stir-fry vigorously for 6 minutes, drain and put aside.

Heat the balance of oil in a separate pan over moderate heat. Add chopped onion and ginger. Stir-fry over high heat for 1 minute, reduce to moderate heat. Pour in the sauce mixture. Stir gently for about $1\frac{1}{2}$ minutes when the sauce will have become quite thick. Add the pork, continue to stir and mix for 2 minutes and then serve.

Soya Pork

3 *lbs belly of pork.*

FOR MARINADE
2 *tablespoons soya bean paste;* $\frac{1}{2}$ *teaspoon salt;* $\frac{1}{4}$ *teaspoon five-spice powder.*

FOR COOKING
3 *tablespoons soya sauce;* 3 *teaspoons sugar;* 4 *tablespoons dry sherry;* $\frac{1}{2}$ *pint water;* 1 *medium-sized onion;* 2 *slices root ginger.*

Preparation
Clean and cut pork through skin into 4 pieces. Rub with bean paste and sprinkle and rub with five-spice powder and salt. Leave to marinate for 2 hours.

Cooking
Heat ingredients for cooking in a heavy pan. Bring to boil and add the pork. As soon as the contents reboil, reduce heat to very low and leave to cook for $1\frac{1}{2}$ hours (insert an asbestos sheet under the pan), turning the pork every half hour. By this time all the liquid should have evaporated.

Serving
Slice the pork through the skin into thin slices (approximately $2\frac{1}{2}'' \times 2''$) each piece to have skin, fat and lean. Serve hot or cold.

Steamed Pork Pudding

3 *lbs belly of pork;* 2 *medium-sized onions;* 2 *slices root ginger.*

FLAVOURING INGREDIENTS

3 *tablespoons soya sauce;* $\frac{1}{2}$ *teaspoon salt;* 2 *teaspoons sugar;*
2 *tablespoons soya bean paste;* 1 *teaspoon bean curd cheese;* 3
tablespoons dry sherry; 3 *tablespoons chopped salted greens or
salted cabbage;* 3 *tablespoons chicken broth.*

Preparation

Boil pork for 10 minutes. Cool and cut pork through skin into
pieces $1\frac{1}{2}''$ long and 2" wide and so that each piece has skin on top
followed by fat and lean below. Place the pork pieces skin downwards in a fireproof bowl. Chop the onion and ginger and place
them on top of the pork. Mix the flavouring ingredients in a
bowl, and spoon them evenly on top.

Cooking

Place the fireproof bowl in a steamer and steam steadily for 2
hours.

Serving

When ready turn the pork out from the bowl into a deep-sided
dish and serve. The smooth pork skin will then be facing up and
should be so soft that it is regarded in China as a meat-jelly. This
dish is supreme with rice.

Egg-Flower Pork

$\frac{3}{4}$ *lb lean pork;* 1 *cup (breakfast) shredded bamboo shoots;* 3
tablespoons 'wood-ear' fungi (soaked in water for 1 *hour, rinsed
and cleaned);* 1 *teaspoon salt;* 3 *eggs;* 2 *tablespoons chicken broth;*
2 *tablespoons dry sherry;* 1 *tablespoon soya sauce;* 1 *teaspoon
gourmet powder;* 1 *teaspoon sesame oil;* 2 *tablespoons vegetable
oil;* 2 *tablespoons lard;* 2 *stalks spring onion* (1" *segments*).

Preparation

Cut pork into slices and then again into double matchstick-sized
strips. Sprinkle with half the salt. Beat eggs together in a bowl
with the remaining salt.

Cooking

Heat vegetable oil in a frying pan. Add pork and stir-fry over high heat for 3 minutes. Remove with a perforated spoon, put aside and keep warm. Add fungi and bamboo shoots into the pan. Stir-fry together for 2 minutes and put aside.

Add lard to the pan. When it has all melted pour in the beaten egg. Reduce the heat and wait until the egg sets, then break it up into a dozen pieces. Return the pork, bamboo shoots and fungi into the pan. Add spring onion and gourmet powder, pour in the broth, soya sauce and sherry. Stir-fry together for $1\frac{1}{2}$ minutes. Sprinkle with sesame oil and serve in a well-heated dish.

Soft-Fried Sliced Pork

1 *lb pork (leg); 2 eggs; 4 tablespoons cornflour; 5 tablespoons vegetable oil; 4 tablespoons chicken broth; $\frac{1}{4}$ teaspoon salt; $\frac{1}{2}$ teaspoon gourmet powder.*

FOR DIP
$\frac{1}{2}$ *tablespoon peppercorns; 2 tablespoons salt.*

Preparation

Slice pork into thin pieces approximately 2″ long and $1\frac{1}{2}$″ wide. Beat eggs in a bowl, add cornflour and mix into a consistent batter. Dip the sliced pork in the batter. Mix salt and gourmet powder with chicken broth in a small bowl.

Cooking

Heat oil in a large frying pan over high heat until very hot. Add pieces of pork and spread them out over the pan. Stir-fry for 2 minutes over high heat. Add seasoned chicken broth and continue to stir-fry for 1–$1\frac{1}{2}$ minutes until all liquid has dried up. Arrange on a well heated dish.

Serving

Heat peppercorns on a dry pan until slightly brown. Crush in a mortar. Add and mix with salt. Divide the 'salt-pepper' into two lots and put in small sauce dishes for use as dips.

Long-Simmered Beef

4 lbs beef (shin); 4 tablespoons vegetable oil; 3 medium-sized onions; 3 slices root ginger; 2 cloves garlic; 1 tablespoon dried tangerine peel; 1 tablespoon sugar; ½ teaspoon salt; 4 tablespoons soya sauce.

Preparation
Cut beef with sharp knife into 1½" cubes, onion into quarters. Soak tangerine peel in water for half an hour. Crush garlic.

Cooking
Heat oil in a large saucepan. When very hot add beef and turn and fry in the oil for 5–6 minutes over high heat, until slightly brown. Reduce the heat and pour in a kettleful of boiling water. Pour away all the oil and water.

Transfer beef to a heavy saucepan. Pour in sufficient water to cover (about 1½–2 pints). Bring contents to boil, and reduce heat to low. Add onion, ginger, garlic, tangerine peel, salt, sugar and soya sauce. Insert an asbestos sheet under the pan, and leave to simmer for 2½ hours under cover over very low heat, turning beef over every half an hour. Serve in a tureen or a deep-sided dish.

Quick-Fried Sliced Lamb with Spring Onion (or Young Leeks)

1 lb lamb (leg); 6 stalks spring onion; 2 cloves garlic; 4 tablespoons vegetable oil; 1 teaspoon sesame oil.

FOR MARINADE
2 tablespoons soya sauce; ¼ teaspoon salt; 1 teaspoon sugar; 2 teaspoons vinegar; pepper (to taste but generous); 2 tablespoons dry sherry.

Preparation
Slice lamb into thin slices approximately 2" long and 1" wide. Cut onion into 2" segments (use green parts). Crush garlic. Mix all

the marinade ingredients in a bowl. Add lamb and mix well with marinade. Leave to season for half an hour.

Cooking
Heat oil in a large frying pan. When very hot add marinated lamb and all the other ingredients at once. Stir-fry vigorously over high heat for $2\frac{1}{2}$ minutes and serve on a well-heated dish.

Quick-Fried Shredded Beef with Onion

1 *lb beef steak;* 3 *medium-sized onions (or 2 large ones);* $\frac{1}{2}$ *teaspoon vegetable oil;* $\frac{3}{4}$ *tablespoon cornflour;* 3 *tablespoons chicken broth;* $\frac{1}{2}$ *teaspoon gourmet powder.*

FOR MARINADE
2 *tablespoons soya sauce;* $\frac{1}{4}$ *teaspoon salt;* 2 *teaspoons sugar;* 2 *tablespoons sherry;* 2 *slices root ginger.*

Preparation
Shred beef with a sharp knife into double matchstick-sized strips. Mix all the ingredients of the marinade together in a bowl. Mix in the beef and marinate for 15 minutes.

Cut onion into thin slices. Mix cornflour with cold chicken broth and gourmet powder.

Cooking
Heat oil in a large frying pan. When very hot add onion, sprinkle with salt, and stir-fry over high heat for 2 minutes. Add the beef, spreading it out evenly over the pan to stir-fry with the onion for 2 minutes. Pour in the cornflour mixture. Continue to stir-fry for $\frac{1}{2}$ minute and serve (on well-heated dish).

Long-Simmered Mutton

4 *lbs mutton;* 3 *medium-sized onions;* 3 *slices root ginger;* 2 *tablespoons dried tangerine peel;* 2 *cloves garlic;* 2 *stalks spring onion (1" segments);* 1 *teaspoon sesame oil;* 6 *tablespoons soya*

sauce; $\frac{1}{2}$ teaspoon salt; 3 teaspoons sugar; 4 tablespoons dry sherry; 2 tablespoons vinegar.

Preparation

Cut mutton with sharp knife into $1\frac{1}{2}''$ cubes. Parboil in boiling water for 3 minutes and drain. Soak tangerine peel in water for $\frac{1}{2}$ hour. Crush garlic.

Cooking

Place mutton in a casserole. Add $1\frac{1}{2}$ pints of water and all ingredients, except spring onions and sesame oil. Insert casserole into a pre-heated oven at 400 degrees (Regulo 6) for 15 minutes. Reduce heat to 300 degrees (Regulo 1) and leave to cook for $2\frac{1}{4}$ hours. Uncover and sprinkle contents with sesame oil and spring onion. Put back on direct heat, bring contents to boil and serve in the casserole.

Stir-Fried Sliced Beef with Tomato

1 lb beef steak; 6 medium-sized tomatoes; $\frac{1}{2}$ teaspoon salt; 3 tablespoons vegetable oil; $\frac{1}{2}$ teaspoon gourmet powder; 3 teaspoons cornflour (blended in 2 tablespoons chicken broth); 1 tablespoon dry sherry; 2 tablespoons chopped spring onion (use green part).

FOR MARINADE

2 tablespoons soya sauce; $\frac{1}{4}$ teaspoon salt; 2 teaspoons sugar; 2 slices root ginger (chop into fine mince); pepper to taste; 1 tablespoon sherry.

Preparation

Skin tomatoes and cut into quarters. Slice beef with sharp knife against the grain into thin slices $1\frac{1}{2}''$ long and $1''$ wide. Mix all the marinating ingredients in a bowl. Add beef and mix well, leaving to marinate for 15 minutes.

Cooking

Heat 2 tablespoons oil in a frying-pan. When very hot add the marinated beef, and stir-fry vigorously over high heat for 1½ minutes. Remove and keep hot.

Add remainder oil into the pan. Pour in the tomato, sprinkle with salt and stir-fry steadily for 1½ minutes. Return the beef into the pan. Add the blended cornflour, sprinkle with gourmet powder, sherry and chopped spring onion. Continue to stir-fry over high heat for 1 minute and serve on a well-heated serving dish.

VEGETABLE DISHES

蔬菜

Red-Cooked Cabbage

1 2lb Chinese cabbage (Savoy cabbage or celery); 4 tablespoons vegetable oil; 3 tablespoons soya sauce; ¼ teaspoon salt; 1 slice root ginger; 6 tablespoons chicken broth; ½ teaspoon gourmet powder; 3 teaspoons sugar.

Preparation
Clean and remove the root of the cabbage. Cut cabbage into quarters and then cut each quarter into four. Chop ginger into small-grained pieces.

Cooking
Heat oil in a large frying pan. When hot add ginger and cabbage, sprinkle with salt and stir-fry over high heat for 2 minutes, until all the vegetable is well-covered with oil. Add soya sauce and broth, pouring them evenly over the cabbage. Add gourmet powder and sugar. Turn the vegetable over 2–3 times. Place a lid over the pan, and leave to cook over low heat for 7–8 minutes. (In a Western kitchen it would be an advantage to add 1 tablespoon butter and break ½–1 chicken stock cube over the vegetable during the second stage of cooking. No gourmet powder would then be required.) Serve in a deep-sided dish.

White-Cooked Cabbage

1 2lb cabbage (Savoy cabbage or celery); 4 tablespoons vegetable oil; 1 slice root ginger; 1½ teaspoons salt; 6 tablespoons chicken broth (or bone broth); ½ teaspoon gourmet powder; 3 teaspoons sugar; 1 tablespoon dried shrimps (soak for ½ hour); 6 tablespoons milk (or 3 tablespoons cream); pepper (to taste).

Preparation
Clean and remove the root of the cabbage. Cut cabbage into quarters, and each quarter into fours. Chop ginger into small grains.

Cooking
Heat oil in a large saucepan. Add salt and ginger. Stir and add cabbage. Stir-fry over high heat for 2 minutes until all the vegetable is well-covered with oil. Add Shrimps, chicken broth, sugar and gourmet powder. Stir gently a few times, and allow the contents to cook under cover over moderate heat for 5 minutes. Add the milk or cream, and allow the contents to continue cooking gently under cover for another 3–4 minutes. Sprinkle with pepper (to taste), and serve. (In a Western kitchen, it might be an advantage to use 1 tablespoon less oil and to finish off by adding 1 tablespoon butter and an extra tablespoon or two of cream before dishing out.)

Hot Sour and Sweet Chinese Cabbage

1 1½–1¾lb Chinese cabbage (Savoy cabbage or celery); ½ teaspoon salt; 3 tablespoons vegetable oil; 2 red chilli pepper.

FOR SAUCE
1½ tablespoons cornflour (blended in 3 tablespoons water); 1½ tablespoons soya sauce; 2 tablespoons vinegar; 3 teaspoons sugar; 1 tablespoon tomato puree; 1 tablespoon dry sherry.

Preparation
Clean and remove the root and outer leaves of the cabbage. Chop the selected parts into pieces 2" by 1" in size.

Shred chilli pepper, discarding pips. Mix all the ingredients for the sauce in a bowl.

Cooking
Heat oil in a large saucepan over high heat. Add chilli pepper and stir-fry for half a minute. Add cabbage, sprinkle with salt and continue to stir-fry for 2 minutes. Close the lid of the saucepan, reduce heat to low and leave to cook for 3 minutes. Take off the lid and pour in the sauce mixture. Increase the heat to high. Stir-fry for 3 minutes and serve.

The cabbage is called 'Sour and Sweet' rather than the ususal 'Sweet and Sour' because it is more sour than sweet; besides it is hotted up by the small amount of chilli pepper.

Casserole of Chinese Cabbage

1 3lb Chinese cabbage (or Savoy cabbage or celery); 6 medium-sized Chinese dried mushrooms; 1 or 2 slices of ham; 1½ teaspoons salt; 1 tablespoon dried shrimps; ½ teaspoon gourmet powder (or chicken-stock cube); 2 tablespoons dry sherry; 1 tablespoon chicken fat; 1½ pints chicken broth.

Preparation
Clean, remove root and outer leaves of the cabbage. Cut it into quarters vertically, and then horizontally three times. Cut ham into pieces 2" by 1½" in size. Soak dried shrimps and mushrooms in water for 30 minutes (remove mushroom stems).

Cooking
Place cabbage in a casserole. Sprinkle with salt. Pour in the chicken broth, sprinkle with shrimps and place the ham and mushrooms (as far as possible) on top of the cabbage. Place the casserole in a pre-heated oven at 400 degrees (Regulo 5) for 10 minutes. Reduce the heat to 325 degrees (Regulo 2) for 20 minutes. Add gourmet powder (or stock cube) sherry and chicken fat. Return the casserole to the oven for a further 20 minutes. Serve in the casserole.

Fu-Yung Cauliflower

1 *medium-sized cauliflower;* 1 *teaspoon salt;* 2 *tablespoons vegetable oil;* $\frac{1}{4}$ *pint chicken broth;* 1–2 *tablespoons chopped ham.*

FOR FU-YUNG SAUCE

2 *egg whites;* 3 *teaspoons cornflour (blended in* 3 *tablespoons water);* 2 *tablespoons minced chicken;* $\frac{1}{2}$ *teaspoon gourmet powder.*

Preparation

Remove the root of the cauliflower and break it into individual flowerets. Beat the ingredients for the Fu-Yung sauce together with a rotary beater for 1 minute.

Cooking

Heat oil in a saucepan. Add cauliflower, sprinkle with salt and stir-fry over high heat for 2 minutes. Pour in the chicken broth and leave to cook under cover for 4–5 minutes over moderate heat. Pour in the Fu-Yung mixture slowly and evenly. Stir gently. Turn the cauliflower over in the sauce. Sprinkle with chopped ham and serve.

Fu-Yung Green Peas

Repeat the preceding recipe, substituting green peas (frozen peas can be used) for cauliflower, except that the length of cooking can be somewhat reduced; the frying can be reduced from 2 minutes to $1\frac{1}{2}$ minutes and cooking in broth from 5 minutes to 3 minutes. Otherwise all the procedure and the quantities are the same.

Steamed Spinach (or 'Spinach Pudding')

$\frac{3}{4}$ *lb minced spinach;* 3 *eggs;* $1\frac{1}{2}$ *teaspoons salt;* 1 *teaspoon gourmet powder (or* 1 *chicken-stock cube);* 1 *pint cold chicken broth;* $1\frac{1}{2}$ *tablespoons lard.*

Preparation

Beat eggs in a large basin for 10 seconds with a fork. Add broth, salt and gourmet powder and blend them together. Add spinach and mix well.

Rub and line the inside of another basin with a layer of lard. Pour the spinach mixture into the basin.

Cooking
Place the basin in a steamer, and steam for 30 minutes. When ready, turn the 'Spinach Pudding' out on a dish and serve.

Plain-Fried Spinach

1¼ lbs spinach; 2 slices root ginger; 1 clove garlic (crushed); 3 tablespoons soya sauce; 2 tablespoons chicken broth; 2 teaspoons sugar; ½ teaspoon gourmet powder (or ½ chicken-stock cube); 4 tablespoons vegetable oil.

Preparation
Clean spinach thoroughly. Remove stems and coarser leaves.

Cooking
Heat oil in a large saucepan. Add ginger and garlic to stir-fry for ¼ minute. Add spinach, turn and mix with the oil for 2 minutes over high heat until all the vegetables are well-lubricated. Add soya sauce, broth, sugar and gourmet powder and continue to stir-fry over high heat for 2½ more minutes. Serve in a well-heated dish.

Plain-Fried Spring Greens (or Broccoli)

Both spring greens and broccoli can be 'plain-fried' in the same way as spinach in the previous recipe. The only difference is that both spring greens and broccoli are tougher vegetables and need longer cooking. Accordingly the chicken broth added is increased, in both cases, from 2 tablespoons to 6 tablespoons and the second period of stir-frying is changed to 4–6 minutes of simmering over moderate heat under cover. In both cases the roots and large stems of the vegetables should be removed and discarded. (The greens would normally require a couple of minutes' less cooking than the broccoli.)

Sweet-and-Sour Cucumber Skin

1 *large long cucumber;* 1 *red chilli pepper;* ½ *teaspoon salt;* 2 *tablespoons vegetable oil.*

FOR SAUCE

3 *tablespoons sugar;* 3 *tablespoons vinegar;* 2 *tablespoons soya sauce;* 1½ *tablespoons tomato puree;* 1½ *tablespoons sherry;* 1 *tablespoon cornflour (blended in 2 tablespoons water).*

Preparation
Clean and cut cucumber in segments approximately 2–2½″ long. Remove about 2″ diameter of its central core, leaving an outside wall of about ¼–½″ thickness. Slice the wall lengthwise into ½″ wide strips.
  Mix all the sauce ingredients in a bowl and blend well.
  Cut and shred pepper, removing pips.

Cooking
Heat oil in a large frying pan. Add chilli pepper, Stir-fry over moderate heat for ½ minute. Add cucumber strips, sprinkle with salt and continue to stir-fry gently over moderate heat for 2 minutes. Pour in the sauce mixture and continue to stir-fry for 1½ minutes. Can be served either hot or cold.

Mustard Cabbage

1½ *lb Chinese cabbage (or Savoy cabbage);* 2–3 *teaspoons mustard powder;* ½ *teaspoon salt;* 2 *tablespoons soya sauce;* 1 *tablespoon vinegar;* 2 *tablespoons lard.*

Preparation
Clean and slice cabbage slantwise into strips 3″ by ½″ in size. Mix mustard (blended with 2 tablespoons water) with salt, soya sauce and vinegar in a basin.

Cooking

Boil cabbage in a pan of boiling water for 2 minutes and drain.

Heat lard in another saucepan. When it has completely melted add cabbage, turn around and mix a few times. Pour in the sauce mixture. Mix gently, and leave to simmer over low heat for a couple of minutes and serve.

This is another one of those dishes which can be served either hot or cold. It is excellent when there are a lot of meat items on the table.

Sweet-and-Sour Stuffed Tomato

6 large firm tomatoes; 4 tablespoons vegetable oil.

FOR STUFFING

3 tablespoons minced pork; 3 tablespoons chopped shrimps; 2 egg whites; $\frac{1}{2}$ teaspoon salt; $\frac{1}{2}$ teaspoon gourmet powder; 2 teaspoons cornflour; 1 tablespoon sherry.

FOR SAUCE

2 tablespoons sugar; 2 tablespoons vinegar; 2 tablespoons soya sauce; 2 tablespoons sherry; 1 tablespoon cornflour (blended in 2 tablespoons water); 3 tablespoons chicken broth.

Preparation

Slice each tomato into half. Scoop about half the inside out but leave the skin firm.

Beat egg whites with a rotary beater for $\frac{1}{2}$ minute and mix them with the other ingredients for the stuffing into a paste. Spread $\frac{1}{2}$–$\frac{3}{4}$ tablespoons of stuffing into each half of tomato.

Mix all the ingredients for the sauce in a bowl.

Cooking

Heat oil in a large flat frying pan. Tilt the pan so that the whole surface of the pan is well-covered with oil. Place the stuffed tomatoes on it one by one, stuffing-side down.   Cook over moderate heat for 3 minutes. Turn the tomatoes over carefully with a slice, and heat the other side for 1 minute. Transfer the tomatoes to a well-heated dish and keep hot (still with the stuffing-side up).

Meanwhile, pour the sauce mixture into the frying pan. Stir and heat for $1\frac{1}{2}$ minutes, when the sauce should have thickened. Pour over the stuffed tomatoes and serve.

Fried Bean Curd with Mushrooms

4 cakes of bean curd; 6 Chinese dried mushrooms; 4 tablespoons minced pork; $\frac{1}{2}$ teaspoon salt ; 1 tablespoon chopped onion; 3 tablespoons vegetable oil; 4 tablespoons mushroom water.

FOR SAUCE

2 tablespoons soya sauce; $1\frac{1}{2}$ teaspoons sugar; 3 tablespoons chicken broth; 3 tablespoons mushroom water; $\frac{1}{2}$ teaspoon gourmet powder; $\frac{3}{4}$ tablespoon cornflour (blended in 2 tablespoons water).

Preparation

Cut each bean-curd cake into 8 pieces. Soak mushrooms in $\frac{1}{2}$ bowlful of water for half an hour, the bowl being the size of an ordinary rice bowl. Press the mushrooms into the water by weighing down with a small saucer.) Retain water for later use. Remove stems and slice each mushroom into four.

Mix all the ingredients for the sauce in a bowl. Blend well.

Cooking

Heat oil in a large frying pan. Add onion, pork and mushrooms, sprinkle with salt and stir-fry for 2 minutes over high heat. Pour in the mushroom water and add the pieces of bean curd. Spread the latter evenly over the pan and turn them around gently for 2 minutes, over moderate heat. Pour in the sauce mixture. As the latter thickens turn the bean curd in the sauce for 3–4 minutes. Serve on a dish or in a bowl.

Braised Bean Curds

4 cakes of bean curds; 1 egg; 2 tablespoons flour; 4 tablespoons vegetable oil; 4 dried mushrooms (soaked for $\frac{1}{2}$ hour and de-stemmed; keep mushroom water).

FOR SAUCE
   2 tablespoons soya sauce; 2 tablespoons shrimp meat; ½ pint chicken
   broth; 2 teaspoon gourmet powder; 1½ tablespoons cornflour
   (blended in 3 tablespoons water); 2 tablespoons sherry.

Preparation
Beat egg and make a batter with flour and 2 tablespoons water.
Cut each bean-curd cake in half and dip each piece in the batter.
   Mix all the ingredients for the sauce in a bowl.

Cooking
Heat oil in a large flat frying pan. When hot lower the pieces of
bean curd into the oil and spread them over the pan. Fry each side
of the curd for about half a minute (3 minutes for eight sides over
moderate heat). Turn them over gently so that they do not break.
Remove the bean curds with a slice and keep warm.
   Add mushrooms into the pan. Stir-fry in the remaining oil
for 1 minute over high heat. Add 4–5 tablespoons mushroom
water and continue to stir-fry for one more minute. Pour the
sauce mixture into the pan. Stir until it thickens. Return the bean
curds to the pan. Lower the heat to a simmer. Turn and heat the
bean curds in the sauce for 5–6 minutes and serve in a bowl.

FISH AND SEAFOODS

魚蝦

The average Peking household does not appear to eat much fish.
Judged by the standard of the coastal southerners, the range of
seafoods in Peking is very limited. There is not much more than
the seasonal crabs and giant prawns from the Gulf of Chilli (the
latter are now becoming widely-known in Europe). 'Carp from
the Yellow River', a well-known culinary item in the North,
seems to appear only at banquets. This lack probably reflects the
absence of adequate or effective refrigeration in the past, which

made the transport of fish and seafood hazardous; it also reflects the fact that Peking is essentially continental in character. The dry winds from the interior seem always to predominate over the moisture-laden sea breezes; yet the coast is barely a hundred miles away.

Braised Fish (Carp, Bream, etc.)

1 fish (2–3 lbs); 2 tablespoons flour; 1 teaspoon salt; vegetable oil for deep-frying; 2 tablespoons bean paste; 1½ tablespoons lard; 2 tablespoons soya sauce; 2 slices root ginger; 3 teaspoons sugar; 2 tablespoons sherry; 2 stalks spring onion (1" segments); ¼ pint chicken broth.

Preparation
Clean fish thoroughly inside and out. Slash the fish on either side at intervals of 1" to the depth of a ¼" and 2–3" in length. Rub with salt and flour.

Cooking
Heat oil in the deep-fryer. When very hot lower the fish to deep-fry in it for 3 minutes on either side (6 minutes in all) and drain.

Heat lard in another frying pan. Add bean paste, soya sauce, ginger, sugar and stir-fry over moderate heat for 1½ minutes. Add spring onion, sherry and broth. Stir for half a minute and when the mixture starts to boil place the fish in it and cover the pan with a lid. After 3–4 minutes turn the fish over and simmer for another 3–4 minutes, when the liquid should have been reduced to half. Serve in a deep-sided dish.

Braised Fish Steak (dry)

1½ lbs fish (carp, pike, eel, etc); ½ teaspoon salt; 2 tablespoons soya sauce; 1½ tablespoons cornflour (blended with 2 tablespoons water); 1 tablespoon chopped onion; 2 slices root ginger (chopped); 1 tablespoon vinegar; 2 tablespoons sherry; 2 teaspoons sugar; 2 tablespoons chicken broth; 3 tablespoons lard.

Fish and Seafoods

Preparation
Slice fish along the grain into pieces $1\frac{1}{2}''$ long and $2''$ wide. Mix
salt, soya sauce and cornflour in a basin. Rub the mixture onto the
fish.

Cooking
Heat lard in a frying pan. When hot and well-spread over the pan
add the fish to fry for 4 minutes (2 minutes on either side). Remove and drain.
 Into the remaining fat in the pan add onion and ginger and
stir-fry over high heat for 1 minute. Pour in the chicken broth,
vinegar, sherry and sugar. Stir with a metal spoon until the mixture boils. Return the pieces of fish into the pan. Turn them around
in the sauce until the latter is virtually dried. It should do so over
the high heat within 2–3 minutes. Serve on a well-heated dish.

Plain Fried Shrimps in Hot Sauce

 1 lb shrimp meat; $\frac{1}{2}$ teaspoon salt; 1 egg; 2 tablespoons cornflour; 3 tablespoons vegetable oil.

FOR SAUCE
 1 tablespoon chopped onion; 1 slice root ginger (chopped); 2
tablespoons soya sauce; 2 tablespoons chicken broth; 1 tablespoon
sherry; 1 tablespoon tomato puree; $1\frac{1}{2}$ teaspoons chilli sauce; 1
tablespoon vinegar; 2 teaspoons sugar.

Preparation
Sprinkle shrimps with salt. Beat egg, add cornflour and mix well
into a batter. Pour the batter on the shrimps and mix evenly.

Cooking
Heat oil in a frying pan. When very hot pour in the shrimps and
quickly spread them apart. Stir-fry for 3 minutes over moderate
heat. Remove and keep hot.
 Add onion and ginger into the pan. Stir-fry over moderate
heat for 1 minute in the remaining oil. Pour in all the other

ingredients for the sauce. Stir until the mixture boils. Return the shrimps to the pan. Stir-fry for 2 minutes and serve.

Phoenix-Tail Prawns

Although this is frequently a banquet dish, it is quite often because of its comparatively simple preparation, served for dinner at home.

8 giant prawns (approximately 2 oz per prawn); 1 teaspoon salt; 2 tablespoons sherry; 4 tablespoons flour; 2 eggs; oil for deep-frying.

Preparation
Remove head and shell of prawns except for tail. Remove dark line from backs. Sprinkle and rub with salt and sherry and leave to marinate for half an hour.

Dredge prawns in flour and then dip in beaten egg (except the tail).

Cooking
Heat oil in the deep-fryer. When hot lower four prawns at a time to deep-fry for 3 minutes. Drain and keep hot. When the second lot of prawns have been dried and drained, return both lots for a further minute's deep-frying.

Serving
Serve on a well-heated dish, with salt-pepper mix (1 teaspoon crushed peppercorns and 2 tablespoons salt heated together on a dry pan for 1 minute) and soya-chilli mix (4 tablespoons soya sauce mixed with 1 tablespoon chilli sauce) as dips.

EGG AND SWEET DISHES

蛋類,甜菜

Smooth Runny Egg (or Peking Scrambled Egg)
This is a typical Peking dish, much loved by local rice-eaters.

6 eggs; $\frac{1}{4}$ pint chicken broth; 2 tablespoons cornflour; 2 tablespoons mashed potato; 3 tablespoons chicken fat (or clarified butter); $1\frac{1}{2}$ teaspoons salt; 1 teaspoon gourmet powder; 4 tablespoons vegetable oil; 2 tablespoons chopped ham; 1 tablespoon lard.

Preparation
Beat eggs in a basin with a beater for $\frac{1}{4}$ minute. Blend cornflour with cold chicken broth and pour into the beaten egg. Add chicken fat, potato, salt and gourmet powder. Beat them together with the rotary beater for $\frac{1}{2}$ minute.

Cooking
Pour vegetable oil into a large saucepan. Tilt the pan over moderate heat so that all parts of the pan are well-oiled. Pour away excess oil and pour in the egg-mixture. Stir the mixture with a wooden spoon, over moderate heat. Stir continually until the contents are smooth and thick and seem well-oiled (about 6–7 minutes). Add lard. Stir once more.

Pour the contents into a deep-sided dish, sprinkle with chopped ham and serve.

Steamed Egg with Duck's Fat

3 eggs; $\frac{3}{4}$ pint chicken broth; 2 tablespoon finely chopped duck's fat; 1 teaspoon salt; $\frac{1}{2}$ teaspoon gourmet powder; 1 tablespoon chopped spring onion (green part); 1 tablespoon soya sauce.

Preparation
Beat eggs in a large basin with a rotary beater for $\frac{1}{4}$ minute. Add broth, fat, salt, and gourmet powder. Beat again for $\frac{1}{4}$ minute.

Cooking
Pour the egg-mixture into a deep-sided dish. Place the latter in a steamer and steam steadily (not too vigorously) for 20 minutes.

Sprinkle the now 'savoury custard' with spring onion and soya sauce and serve in the original dish.

'Crab's Rival'

4–5 oz white fish (sole, cod, haddock, etc.); 4 eggs; 3 tablespoons lard; 1 tablespoon chopped spring onion; 1 teaspoon chopped root ginger; ½ teaspoon salt; 1 tablespoon tomato puree.

COOKING SAUCE
2 teaspoons cornflour; 6 tablespoons concentrated chicken broth; 2 tablespoons sherry; ½ teaspoon salt; ½ teaspoon gourmet powder.

Preparation
Cut fish into ½ cubes. Beat egg in a basin for 10 seconds. Put all the ingredients for sauce into a separate basin and beat together for another 10 seconds.

Cooking
Heat lard in a frying pan. Add onion and ginger followed by diced fish. Stir gently together and pour in the beaten egg and sprinkle ½ teaspoon salt over the contents of the pan.

Stir and turn slowly until the egg is just about to set. Pour in the sauce mixture from the basin and continue to stir and turn for another 2 minutes over moderate heat. Sprinkle a few drops of tomato puree into different parts of the egg fish mixture. Turn over a couple of times and serve in a well-heated deep-sided dish.

'Peking Snowballs'

8 egg whites; 1½ tablespoons flour; 1½ tablespoons cornflour; 8 tablespoons sweetened bean paste; vegetable oil for deep-frying; 3 tablespoons caster sugar.

Preparation
Form bean paste into 12 round balls. Beat egg whites until quite

stiff. Mix flour and cornflour together, sprinkle gradually in to the egg white and mix consistently.

Divide the mixture into 12 portions. Wrap each portion around a bean-paste ball to make a larger ball.

Cooking

Heat oil in the deep-fryer. When hot add 6 'snowballs' at a time to fry for $3\frac{1}{2}$ minutes over moderate heat. Turn the balls around as they float. Drain, and fry the second lot.

When both lots are ready, place on a dish, sprinkle with caster sugar and serve.

Peking Drawn-Thread Glazed Apple

6 firm medium-sized apples; 2 eggs; 4 tablespoons flour; oil for deep-frying.

FOR GLAZING SYRUP
5 tablespoons sugar; 2 tablespoons water; 3 tablespoons vegetable oil.

Preparation

Core and peel the apples and cut each into 4–6 pieces. Beat eggs, add flour and blend into a smooth batter. Dip apples in the mixture to take on a coating of batter.

Cooking

Heat oil in the deep-fryer. When very hot, lower ten pieces of apple at a time to deep-fry for $3\frac{1}{2}$ minutes and drain. Repeat until all the pieces of apple are fried.

Place the ingredients for glazing syrup in a large saucepan over moderate heat. Stir with a wooden spoon until the syrup thickens and is about to turn brown. Add the deep-fried apples, turn them quickly in the syrup until each piece is well-covered.

Serving

Transfer the apple pieces to a well-heated and well-greased dish or bowl and bring quickly to the table. Each diner picks the pieces of apple up with his chopsticks and plunges them into a large bowl of iced water. This gives the apple a brittle glaze. As each piece of apple is lifted up before plunging in water, it draws a thread of syrup behind it (like a thread of drawn-glass), hence the name. The sweet crispy encrustation makes biting into the apples a unique sensation.

'Peking Dust'

This is not an indigenous Peking dish but was invented by European expatriates after the First World War. It became well-known and therefore a part of local history. It is included here for the sake of Western nostalgia.

> $1\frac{1}{4}$ *lbs chestnuts;* $\frac{1}{4}$ *teaspoon salt; 5 tablespoons sugar; 1 cup double cream; 2 tablespoons caster sugar.*

Preparation
Score and boil chestnuts in water for 45 minutes. Drain. Cool and shell. Grind chestnuts in a blending machine to a light powder. Add sugar and salt. Continue to blend for a while until well-mixed.

Blend caster sugar with cream.

Serving
Serve in individual portions by forming the chestnut 'dust' into a small mound on each serving plate and topping it with a spoon-ful or two of sweetened cream (the cream can in turn be decorated with a piece of glazed fruit if so desired).

Index

Recipes in italic

173

Index

Index